Leon Brown, backstage, Brooklyn Academy of Music

Pumping Iron
The Art and Sport of Bodybuilding

Written by Charles Gaines
Photographs by George Butler

Designed by Martin Stephen Moskof

Simon and Schuster   New York

Also by Charles Gaines
 Stay Hungry

Also by George Butler (with David Thorne)
 The New Soldier

The authors gratefully acknowledge: permission
to reprint lines from "The Leg," from *Selected
Poems* by Karl Shapiro, copyright 1944 by
Karl Shapiro, published by Random House, Inc.;
and Mr. Joseph Weider of *Muscle Builder
Power* magazine, 21100 Erwin Street, Woodland
Hills, California, for permission to use material
from the magazine.

Published by Simon and Schuster
Rockefeller Center, 630 Fifth Avenue
New York, New York 10020

SBN 671-21898-0 Casebound
SBN 671-21922-7 Paperback
Library of Congress Catalog Card Number: 74-11700

Manufactured in the United States of America

This book is dedicated to the people and sport it describes, and particularly to Joe Disco.

Introduction

I have been involved with bodybuilding in one way or another since I was sixteen years old. I began lifting weights then and have done it lazily and noncompetitively ever since. I have also written about it previously in a different form. This book grew out of that involvement and, specifically, out of a story for *Sports Illustrated* that George Butler and I did in the summer of 1972 on the Mr. East Coast contest which was held in Holyoke, Massachusetts, and won in that year by Leon Brown. Since then we have been to quite a few places tracking bodybuilders, seeing contests and putting together the materials here. If we felt at times a little like 19th-century explorers, it was because we found bodybuilding to be as primeval and unmapped as parts of Labrador. Nobody, we discovered, had been back into it to send out a report on what it was like.

This struck us then as peculiar, and it still does. America is a country of subcultures, and most of them, including ones as esoteric as midget wrestling, pimping and the Roller Derby, have been thoroughly explored and documented. Like those activities, bodybuilding is an obsession, a living (for a few), and a way of life for the people involved in it—a subculture, in a word, with its own values, aesthetics and vocabulary. The fact that it seems to us a far more fascinating and resonant one than any of those other three might sound simply practical for the authors of a book about it, but it is also true. And yet no one had undertaken seriously to describe it. To our knowledge, this is the first book ever on the subject.

In the Middle East bodybuilding is the second most popular spectator sport. There, and in Japan, Australia, the West Indies, South Africa and parts of Europe, its competitions are national events. There are probably a number of reasons why it has never taken hold like that in America, and one of them certainly is that almost since its beginnings here, bodybuilding has advertised itself with consummate tackiness, confining itself to the back pages of pulp magazines and, in the national consciousness, to the same shadowy corners occupied by dildos and raincoat exhibitionists. Unflattering myths developed early here. And the composite picture that seems to have emerged from them, of bodybuilders as narcissistic, coordinatively helpless muscleheads with suspect sexual preferences, has done little to promote the sport.

Part of what we have tried to do is to demonstrate that this is an inaccurate picture. We have also wanted to describe truly something of the sport, art and life of bodybuilding, and to suggest in passing that if you have never been to a good physique contest you have definitely missed something.

But mostly we think of this book as a sort of respectful report from the interior of an interesting, colorful and heretofore ignored region of American life. It does not attempt to be comprehensive, and to anyone who finds himself—or something he knows or represents—skimped or omitted, the authors apologize. What it does attempt to do is to chart, with some accuracy and a proper sense of wonder, the heart of the terrain.

We want to thank our wives, Victoria and Patricia, for their grace and high sense of fun during the process of putting this book together. A lot of other people have been helpful. We are grateful to all of them and would like to acknowledge these especially: Dr. Larry Golding, Ben Weider, Sig Klein, Enrico Natali, Tom Miniechiello, Dietz Heins, Jeri Wentz and Evelyn Blair.

Charles Gaines
George Butler

Pumping Iron

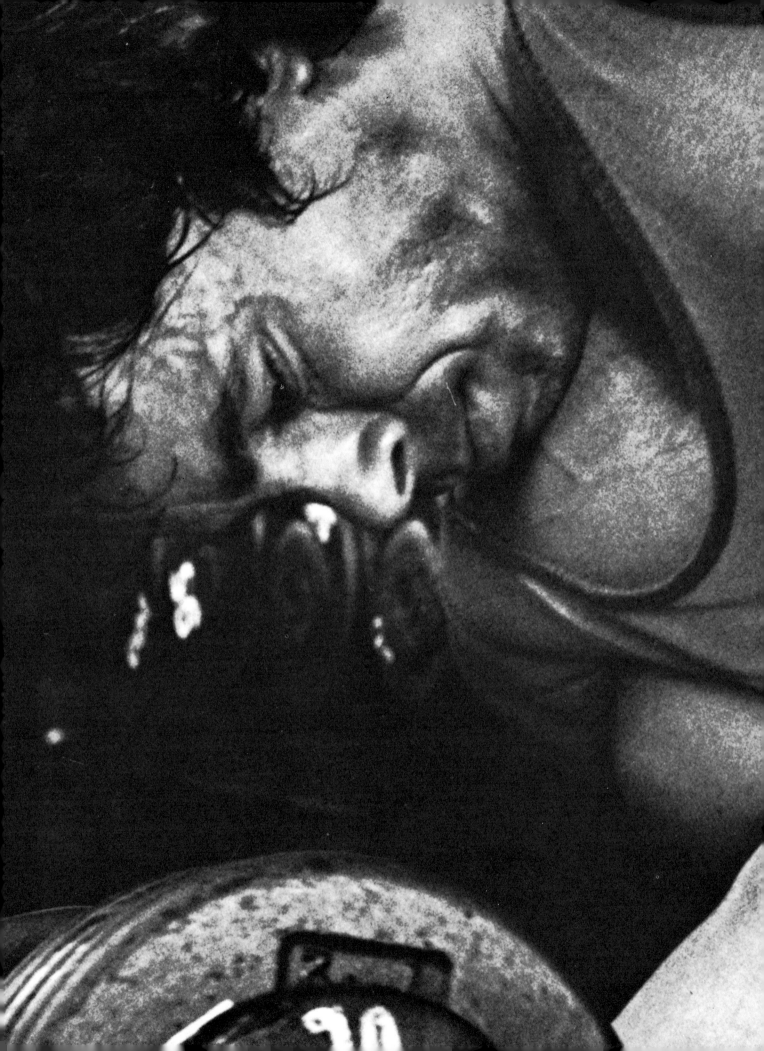

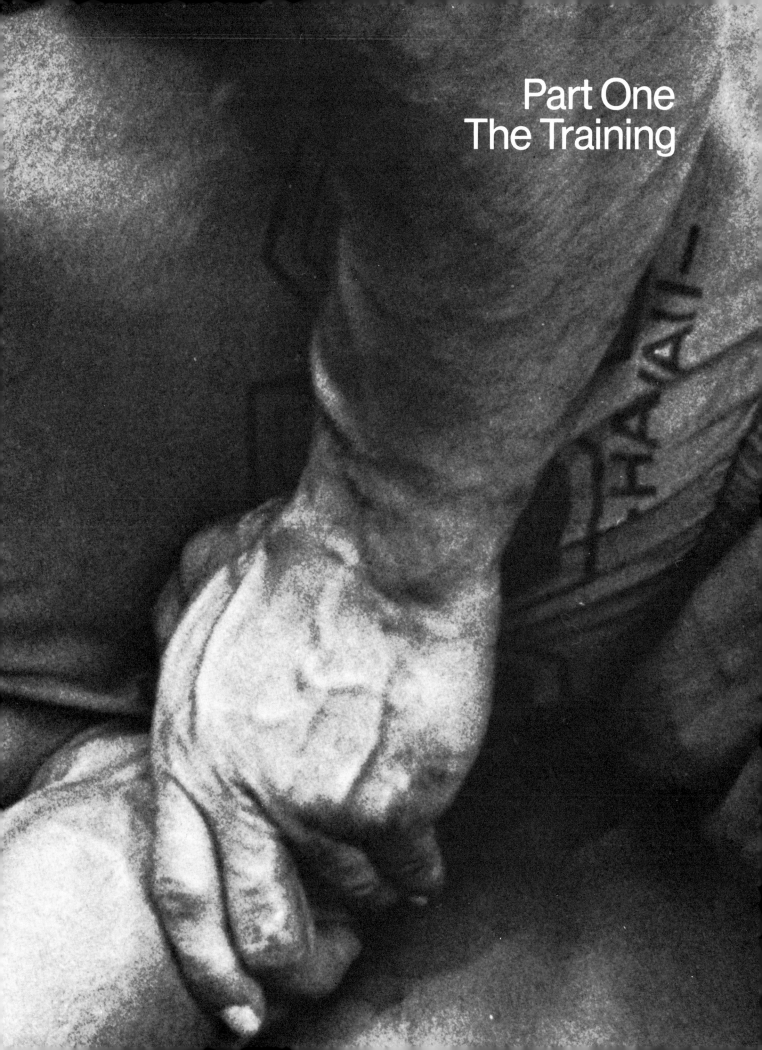

Part One
The Training

"The body, what is it, Father, but a sign
To love the force that grows us, to give back
What in Thy palm is senselessness and mud?"

—Karl Shapiro

"For soule is forme, and doth the bodie make."

—Edmund Spenser

One
Mr. Olympia No. 1

At 10:45 the house lights go down and the Brooklyn Academy of Music falls seriously quiet for the first time all evening. Martin Stader, master of ceremonies and former Mr. Universe, says the following:

"Ladies and Gentlemen, the first contestant in the 1973 Mr. Olympia contest. From France . . . Serge Nubret."

The old-fashioned music-hall curtain is raised, and there, spotlighted on the posing dais in profile to the audience, as underdressed as his introduction, is the massive and fabled Nubian Lion. It is his first appearance in America. The aficionado crowd is reticent at first, busily checking him over as it would a touted European car—part by part, kicking his tires, squinting up at those famous pectorals as though they might have a French accent.

Nubret waits for a moment for the noise level to rise, and then begins with a set of swooping side shots, putting his best up in front of the judges right away—the tiny waist, vacuumed into a comma, the unusually high and well-formed pectorals that slope from his collarbones like hogback ridges, the cantaloupe-sized deltoids. And the arms. Nubret's arms, it is clear, are as dangerous as they are reputed to be: massive, symmetrical, the muscles cleanly divided and balanced. No disappointment there, and the crowd tentatively begins to hype. He does the single-bicep pose with his right arm, keeping his left behind him, fist cocked at the hip in a tricep flex . . . holds it . . . and pivots to face the judges to begin his front shots.

But, with the turn, something mysteriously escapes Nubret's routine; vitality seeps fatally from it like gas from a soufflé.

Serge Nubret

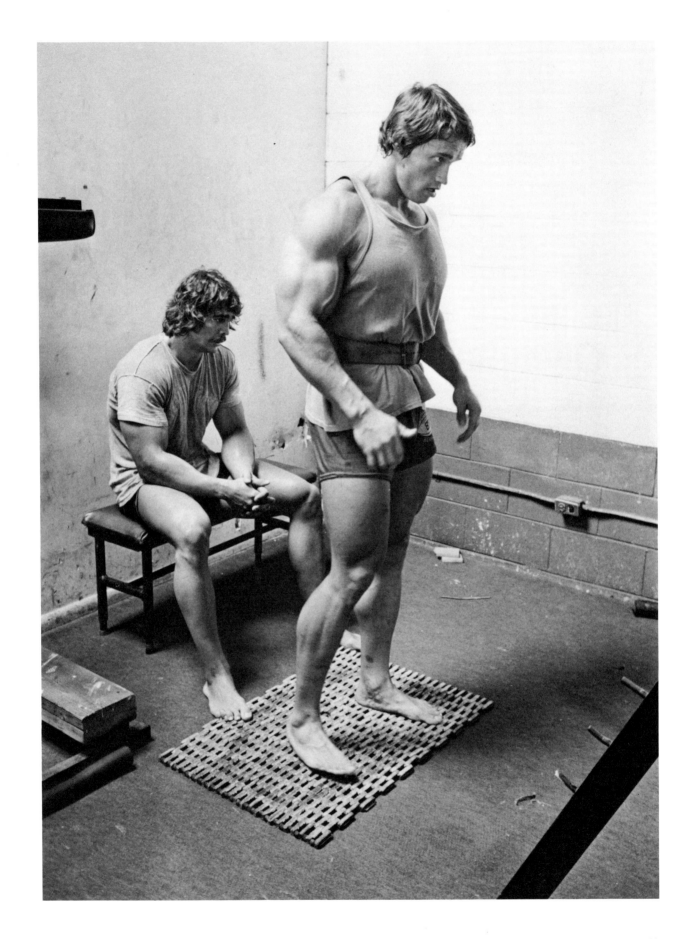

Arnold Schwarzenegger
Mr. Europe, AAU Mr. World, 5
times Mr. Universe, 4 times and
current Mr. Olympia.
26 years old
6'2" tall
240 lbs.
57" chest
22" arms
31" waist
28" thighs
20" calves

At the squat rack, Gold's Gym

Wrist Curls

Franco Columbu
Mr. Italy, Mr. Europe, 3 times
IFBB Mr. Universe, 3 times IFBB
Mr. World
30 years old
5'5" tall
185 lbs.
50" chest
19" arms
30" waist
26" thighs
17½" calves

He has swung into position for most of the favored bodybuilding poses: the double-biceps, the most muscular. It is an instant when he should have the crowd rising to him, the applause and whistles and moans shaping into proper tumult. But something happens, and Nubret's promise, his sense of potential, his mystery, is gone. Bodybuilders call it disappearing. The celebrated weaknesses, his back and legs, suddenly seem to leap into neon. The crowd continues to applaud, but he has lost it. It has gone subtly and irrevocably polite on him.

The rest of his routine is as lackluster as heavy machinery being moved around. He goes through his front and back poses seriously and awkwardly, stumbling occasionally on the dais. One notices a bodybuilder's face at such times, and Nubret's handsome West Indian features remain so composed, so *removed* from the situation, that his expression begins to seem part of the problem. It's as thoroughly joyless and preoccupied as an astronaut's. It is also resigned. He knows he has just kissed off one year's worth of training.

That's how long Serge Nubret has savaged himself for this year's Mr. Olympia contest—ever since the same competition last September in Essen, Germany, where he placed third. And a year is big money to Nubret. In addition to being Mr. France and one of the preeminent bodybuilders in the world, he is a movie and television star in France and the owner of a chain of Parisian gyms. World-class bodybuilding takes more time than a businessman-actor has to give, and, win or lose, this is his last contest. But he wanted this one badly. It is the biggest title in bodybuilding—one for which only the four or five best professional builders in the world can compete—and he wanted it for Guadeloupe, an island that he left twenty-three years ago for France and where he is now an almost completed legend.

For the last twelve months, for three hours each morning, three each afternoon and two each night, Nubret has pushed and pulled maniacally at iron while sustaining a diet that would explode an ordinary metabolism—doing for that renowned chest, for instance, forty sets of twenty benchpresses (pushing 210 pounds off his chest a total of eight hundred times every other day) and ingesting nine pounds of meat, four hundred grams of protein supplement and thirty-two glasses of water *daily*.

It is a slightly crazed schedule. And to support it, it is not hard to imagine Nubret developing, in the late recesses of one of his gyms, where all thought of money and movie fame is banished for a year, the mirthless purpose, the grim sense of do or die, that he brought with him to New York.

Nine AM, two weeks before the contest in New York: a chest, back and leg day at Gold's Gym in Venice Beach, California. Outside, a fog curls down Pacific Avenue, blanking the windows

"Chuck Sipes was strong but I am much stronger than him. Very much stronger than him. All around. Because he was strong on the benchpress. I'm strong in everything. Any kind of movement you can find in a gym, I can beat everybody in it."
—Franco Columbu

Check posing

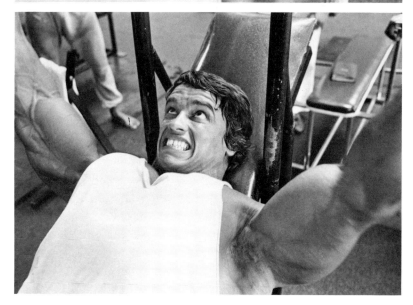

"When I was ten years old I got this thing that I wanted to be the best in something, so I started swimming. I won championships, but I felt I couldn't be the best. I tried it in skiing, but there I felt I didn't have the potential. I played soccer, but I didn't like that too well because there I didn't get the credit alone if I did something special. I just avoided team sports from then on. Then I started weight lifting through the other sports and I enjoyed it the most. I won the Austrian championship in 1964 but I found out I was just too tall. So I quit that and went into bodybuilding. Two years later I found out that that's it—that's what I can be the best in."
——Arnold Schwarzenegger

Pullovers

Benchpresses

and isolating the gym—making its peculiar energy seem singular and lonely as an atom's.

Inside, Nubret's competition, the other two contestants for the Mr. Olympia title, are beginning a morning of their own type of training. Outsized diagrams of railroad cars join in a frieze about the mirrored wall. Beneath them Arnold Schwarzenegger, "the Austrian Oak," is happily pushing 315 pounds twelve times off his supine self. Smooth, flat-back repetitions: the black Olympic bar falls to his chest, pauses, rises, three 45-pound plates, big as manhole covers, jiggling at either end. Schwarzenegger is the current Mr. Olympia. He also happens to be the best bodybuilder alive, and very possibly the most perfectly developed man in the history of the world. He came to this country in 1968 from Graz, Austria, brought over by an American muscle entrepreneur named Joe Weider. When Weider found him, Schwarzenegger had been a competitive swimmer, soccer player, skier, boxer, wrestler, shot-putter and javelin thrower; he had been the weight-lifting champion of Austria and the curling champion of Europe; he was Mr. Europe and Mr. Universe—and he was all of twenty-one years old. Now, at twenty-six, he has won five Mr. Universe titles and the last three Olympias, and he has not lost a contest since 1969. It is a record of total domination in bodybuilding that compares with Pele's in soccer, or Merckyx's in cycling, or Killy's in skiing. That kind of outrageous superiority is always subject to demeaning imputations. And there are people around who will tell you that Schwarzenegger injects himself with silicone, or that he uses truckloads of anabolic steroids. The truth is simply that he was born with more physical talent, is smarter at the sport, and works at it with more joy and fierceness than any other bodybuilder in history. That, and one other thing: he has wanted to be the best at something, the very best, since he was ten years old.

As always there is a knot of people watching him. Three of them, Kent Kuehn from Florida, Denny Gable from Iowa, and I, will follow the set, using progressively lighter weight but sweating more and breathing harder. Kuehn calls it chasing Arnold. This is the fourth set of benchpresses. There will be five more; then there will be five sets of presses on an inclined bench, five sets of dumbbell flyes and two sets of twenty cable flyes—all designed to bulk, shape, striate and clarify the pectoralis muscles of the chest by means of a fearful tearing down of tissue there. At this early moment in the routine I, for one, could testify truly that the tearing down occurs. But as you watch Arnold's fifty-seven-inch chest, which resembles an ordinary man's the way a Waterford punch bowl does a fruit jar, spreading and humping ornately under the weight, you are aware of the ache in your own as someone playing tennis with Rod Laver might be aware of blisters. Pain is growth around here. The men in this room,

Franco Columbu, pumping up

many of them, have come from all over the country just to be able to hurt with Arnold.

There is a quality of festiveness, a strong sense of celebration, at Gold's that you don't find at other gyms. It has to do with pride. Many of the biggest names in bodybuilding are regulars—Franco Columbu, Frank Zane, Dave Draper, Ken Waller. And hotshots from all over the world make annual pilgrimages here. More than half the winners of the three big September contests in New York will come from this one gym, and the people here know it. They know Gold's is where it's at. And they know why. It is mostly because of the six-foot-two-inch, 235-pound Austrian over there doing benchpresses. He attracts the best because he states their case. They come from all over to follow his training, and also because he is the embodied articulation of what they do. The people standing around now watching his chest are looking at *an idea made fact*—a chest carried out of mind to absolute and final form. And there is another thing. Because he is a natural, cleaving as closely to this strange sport-art as a piece of Saran Wrap to a table, to watch him train is to glimpse immediately and vividly what is most real about the development of a body for exhibition. Other bodybuilders can read the true grain of their commitment through him as easily as they can count the divisions of muscle beneath the skin on his chest.

Finished with the set, he stands up, tugging at his shorts, and surveys the gym, his gray eyes prowling for anything new that might have developed. Over by the chinning bar, dressed in a red tank suit and high-topped shoes, doing bent-over rows with three hundred pounds, is his best buddy and the third Mr. Olympia contestant—a massive and puckish Sardinian named Franco Columbu, who looks as if he ought to smoke thin cigars in Italian Westerns. At five feet five inches and 185 pounds, he is one of the strongest men alive for his size, and the only bodybuilder other than Arnold to make his living at it. The two of them travel together all over the world on exhibition tours, but they don't have much to do with each other here in the gym. Arnold yells something to him in German. Franco leers briefly and answers. Both men have an ability to make their slightest gestures seem important, and the whole gym taps into this exchange. These are the two Head Men, each riding his own momentum into the last two weeks of an eight-month blitz for the same title; God knows what they might be saying. But Arnold doesn't continue the conversation. He makes a little circle around the gym, clapping a shoulder here, gibing somebody there— pulling things together. Then he ambles back over to the bench, lies down, and grabs off the new weight like a haunch of turkey.

As the morning progresses there is much laughter, sweating and spillage: messy, boisterous, intent—the weights clanging

like tableware—the activity comes to resemble a medieval feast.
On the floor the shanks of barbells gleam like bones. The other
dozen or so men in the gym struggle and rest to separate rhythms,
yet they are all connected to the same central energy: to the digestion of exercise, the turning of work into themselves. It is a
visible process and a riveting one—much more than vanity, it
is the reason why a bodybuilder studies himself in mirrors.
Watching a muscle after working it, he can *see* the freshly oxygenated blood flooding the tissue, spreading and flushing the
skin, creating the condition known as a pump—the sacramental
engorgement of muscle that is an outward and visible sign of
growth. A pump is the fix and rush of bodybuilding. It produces
a feeling that is wonderfully clearheaded, self-sufficient and
refreshed—as though all the blood were new. The feeling spills
over and fills the gym. The fog at the windows that covers all
of Venice Beach might as well have eaten it; and with it, all
those people out there who don't know a Mr. Olympia from a
Mr. Des Moines. Gold's Gym is buzzed on a pump. Together.
Doing fine.

Two

First there are the big-city gyms—places like Tom Miniechiello's Mid-City in Manhattan and Julie Levine's R & J in Brooklyn, which are two of the best. A few very good bodybuilders like Leon Brown and many others who are not so good have come out of these places. But there is usually a depressing sense of anonymity about them, and a lot of the people there do not look happy while they are working out. A few of them look overtly hostile, as if the energy of the workout were tickling them with violence. Some look unpleasantly lost in themselves. Some just look sad. But practically no one looks happy. You wonder about people who don't look happy while they are working out, because very few things feel better to the body. Whatever the reason, it is only in these big-city gyms that you find many of them.

Then there are the "spas," the fancy health clubs like the ones owned by Jack La Lanne, or like the old Vic Tanney chain, which got very big in the fifties and then went broke. The spas feature individualized training programs, carpeting, pretty chrome weights and a lot of unnecessary reducing machines. They try hard to cater to business and professional types, and they usually don't encourage serious bodybuilding, though a few will play both ends of the street by stacking some black weight off in a room by itself for anyone redneck enough to want to use it. They all glitter, these places. The attendants are usually bulky, smiling people dressed in white uniforms. Very few good bodybuilders come out of "spas."

Almost every YMCA in America has a weight room, and all of the ones I know about (with a few exceptions, like the big Y on Central Park West where the faggots will track you to the

Mid-City Health Studio, Manhattan

27

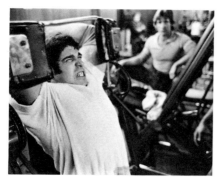

Lou Ferrigno, R and J Studio

"They say we are muscle-bound and freaks. Well, I tell you the truth, man: I never really pay too much attention to these people. The more they talk, that's the more I'm going to continue working out. Because that's the way I feel about it. It's the thing I want to do and I'm going to continue. I don't care what they say. . . . I think that it's a very good thing and I'm going to continue with it as long as the Lord leaves me breath and I have the strength to go along with it. I'm going to be doing it all the time."
—Lawrence Samuel

Pete Caputo, R and J Studio, Brooklyn

shower with their heads down like they were following a spoor) are wonderful places to train. They always have good basic equipment, and you know while you are working out that you can go upstairs afterward and smooth off with a run or some basketball. Y gyms are generally good-humored places. Some of the funniest talk I've ever heard came out of a Y gym I used to go to in Atlanta. At the one I use now there is a stocky, javelin-throwing former Mr. New Hampshire powerlifter named Punky Stewart. Punky Stewart wears red-white-and-blue shoes and a bright-red halter when he works out. He walks in dressed like that, chewing gum very fast, and eyes the Olympic bars lying around like a dog looking at table scraps. Then Punky will start grinning. He grins right through every exercise and everything he says, and when he goes upstairs to shower he is still grinning.

Mike Katz used to use a Y gym in Hartford, Connecticut. Mike is a funny guy and it is easy to imagine that that gym was a very good-humored place. But after he won the IFBB Mr. America contest in 1971, people at the gym started to heavy up with him, so Mike began working out in a garage with just his training partner, Joe Ugolik, and Coach, a nice old guy who helped train Mike and who owned the garage.

George Butler and I were there at Coach's garage one day when Mike and Ugolik were working legs. It was early spring and still cold, so the first thing they did was to fire up an 85,000-BTU torpedo-shaped space heater. The heater made a constant whooshing noise and put out a hard, old-fashioned smell that suited the place. The garage was full of old weights and machines that Coach had made, all of them functional, and arranged precisely around the walls so that there was good space in the middle. Mike and Ugolik began doing leg presses, working from 310 up to 650 pounds in six sets—lying on their backs under the weight, legs spread wide above their chests, letting their thighs come all the way down to their armpits before they pushed up the platform. And Coach stood in the middle of the slowly warming garage watching them use the equipment he had made, and helping by talking up the weight.

"Nice and easy," he told them over and over, rubbing his hands together. "Push it way up. Atta*boy*, Mike. *Way* up, now" —watching them the way you might watch someone you cared about riding a horse you had trained.

The very best places to do bodybuilding, though, are the few gyms run just for bodybuilding by someone who doesn't care particularly about overweight businessmen. These places, like the very best bars, never make all the money they could make, and sometimes they don't make any money at all, which probably accounts for why there are so few of them. I have been in only two of these places. One is gone now. It was in Birming-

29

Bill Pearl at his club in Pasadena

ham, Alabama. Gold's Gym is the other one, and it is doing fine out in Venice. The guy who owns Gold's, I understand, doesn't need the money. The guy who owned the one in Birmingham went broke and moved to Florida. They say Vince Gironda's Gym in North Hollywood is in this category, and George Eifferman's in Las Vegas, and Bob's Gym in Fremont. I don't know; I've never been to those places. Tom Miniechiello's place in New York would be if it weren't for all the unhappy-looking people, and they are not Tommy's fault.

What these places have in common, besides less income than they'd make if they were "spas," are these things: good equipment, good people, good humor and the right feel. The feel of a really good bodybuilding gym has to do with a sense of inevitability of what's done there. If the feel is right, it causes you to believe while you are there that there is nothing in life so worthwhile or fun or exciting as pumping iron.

One person, if he's big enough, can give a place this feel.

The place in Birmingham was called the Magic City Health Club. It was on the second floor of a brick building right in the middle of town. Between sets you could look down through the big picture windows at what was happening out on Second Avenue, and the hurry out there always made you feel glad that you were up where you were with no place to go. In the summer somebody would open the fire-escape door in the back, and the wonderful mustard-and-meat smell from Pete's Hot-Dog Stand would drift through the gym, speeding up the workouts as it started to work on people. There were a lot of big boys using Magic City in those days who stayed hungry and who could flat-handle a hot dog. Eating six or seven after a workout and before dinner just to kick back at that smell was not unusual.

Billy Joe Barrett, two or three times Mr. Birmingham and almost a Mr. Alabama, used Magic City then. And Pee Wee Suits, who might have done something except for his calves. And Richard "Radar" Coe, who could have won just about anything around but came from the Country Club side of the mountain and so couldn't compete. It was a good group and a funny group, but it was Joe Disco who gave the place its feel.

Disco came from Ohio. Maybe. He was twenty-eight or thirty-four. He might have had a master's degree, and been married at one time, and had a lot of money. Nobody really knew, because Disco was creative with his past. It was a part of his art to tinker with it. Of his present, you knew that off and on he managed the health club; that sometimes, when he had money, he drove a sports car and lived in a swank apartment building with a swimming pool; and that other times, when he didn't, he stayed in a rooming house in Five Points and lived off coffee and protein pills. He trained, but not for competition anymore. He might have been a Mr. Universe. He claimed to have invented a revolu-

Coach, Mike Katz and Joe Ugolik, West Hartford, Conn.

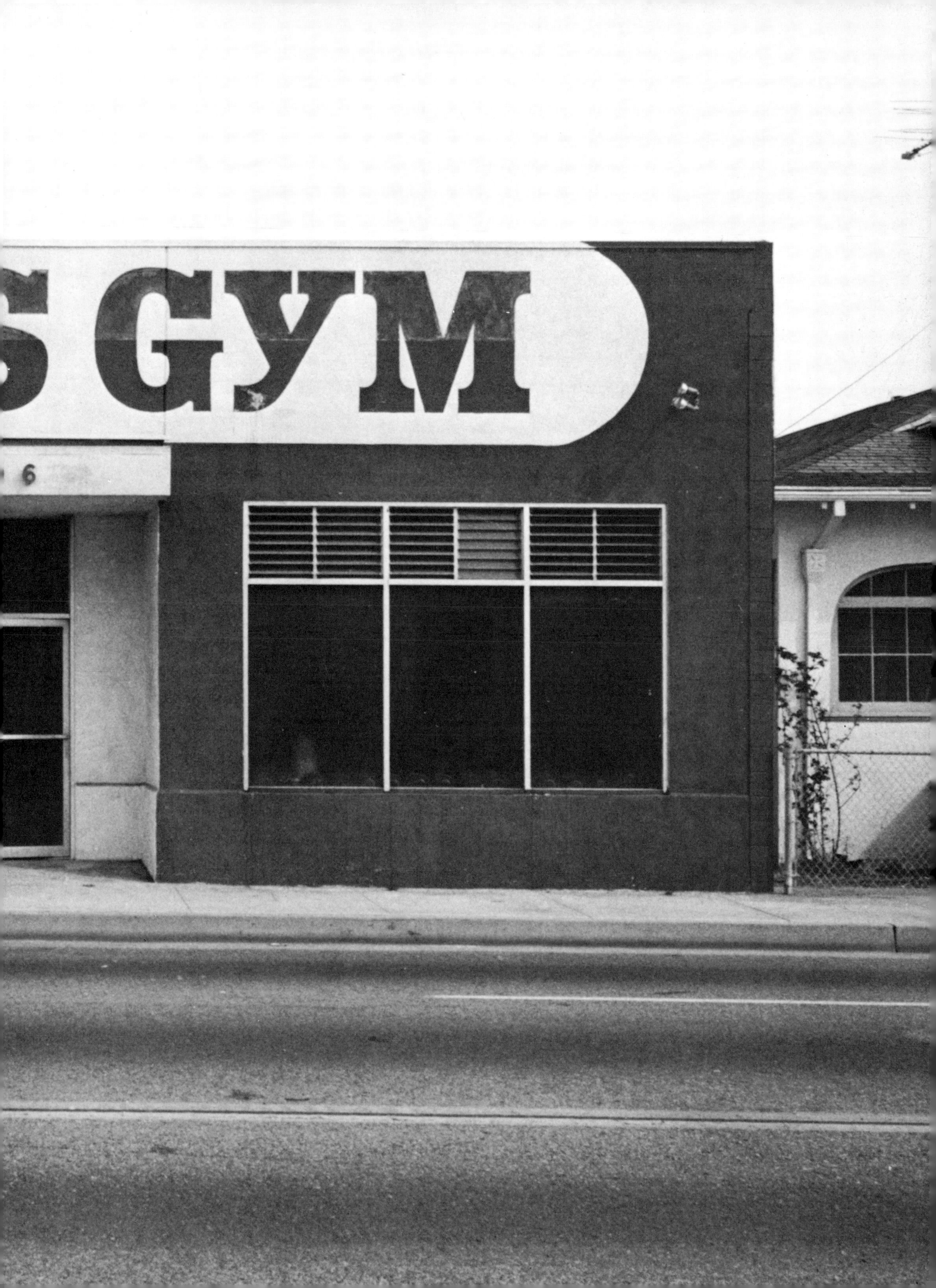
GYM
6

tionary bowling glove and a system for renting towels to high-school gyms, either one of which could make him rich overnight, but he didn't let them out because he didn't want the hassle.

Joe didn't want to get hung on anything outside the gym. The gym was his pivotal place; one half of him was stuck there, like the pointed arm of a compass, and he wanted that other arm free to move. He loved the gym. He relished the work and fun and pump of working out and what it did for you and how it made you feel, and he made everybody else relish it, too—made them feel that nothing else was nearly as important.

That summer and fall of my wife's first pregnancy, just before we left the South, she and I and Joe would walk in the evenings down to Joy Young's Chinese Restaurant for dinner after working out. Joe had her working out, too, downstairs in the ladies' section. The three of us would swing out of Magic City through the warm cottony Alabama dark with Joe talking and with Patricia in the middle, leaning a little to aft, and laughing her fine deep laugh. Heading for egg rolls and sweet-and-sour pork, feeling sinfully clean and brand new and very fresh and clear in the head, we felt on those walks as if we owned the sidewalks. That's the way a really good gym will always make you feel.

Aside from a flashy red, white and blue sign over the door, Gold's Gym is not a very interesting-looking place from the outside. It's a chunky one-story buff-colored building, hunkering so close to Pacific Avenue that three steps out the door puts you into the middle of traffic. But inside it's exactly right. In the back there is a small office and a protein bar. Above them are showers and a locker room. All the rest is gym.

It is a bright, pleasant, uncrowded room with a high ceiling, big enough for fifteen or twenty men to work out at the same time without getting in each other's way. To work out with, there are two or three tons of weight lying around. Dozens of black iron dumbbells are racked in pairs along two walls, ranging in size from 5 pounds up to around 150. There are also barbells whose weights are fixed at various poundages up to a hundred pounds or so, and for anything heavier than that there are three or four Olympic sets.

An Olympic barbell is the basic piece of bodybuilding equipment, as central to it as an iron is to golf. The bar is seven feet long and weighs 45 pounds with the collars. The best ones are made of cadmium steel. Its central section is about the same diameter as a garden hose, and the knurled gripping lengths come into the hands as comfortably as the handle of an old ax. At either end of the bar there is a two-foot section, twice as big in diameter as the shank, onto which the black flanged cast-iron plates are slid. You can get six 45-pound plates on each end of an Olympic bar without the collars. That would bring its weight

Denny Gable, Gold's Gym

I Front
1. Deltoid
2. Pectoralis Major
3. Biceps
4. Serratus Magnus
5. Rectus Abdominis
6. External Obliques
7. Rectus Femoris
8. Vastus Externus
9. Vastus Internus

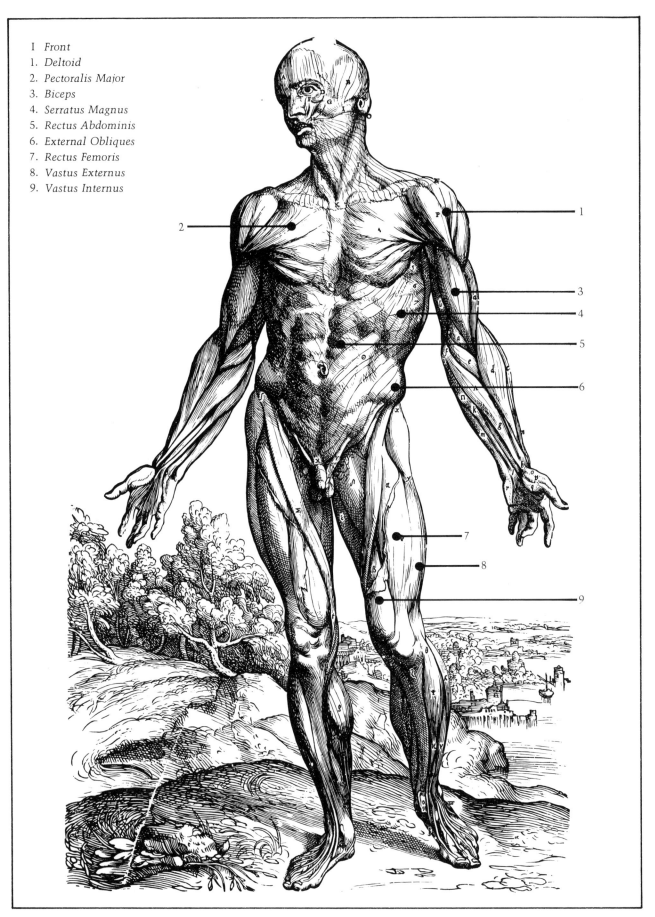

2

1

3

4

5

6

7

8

9

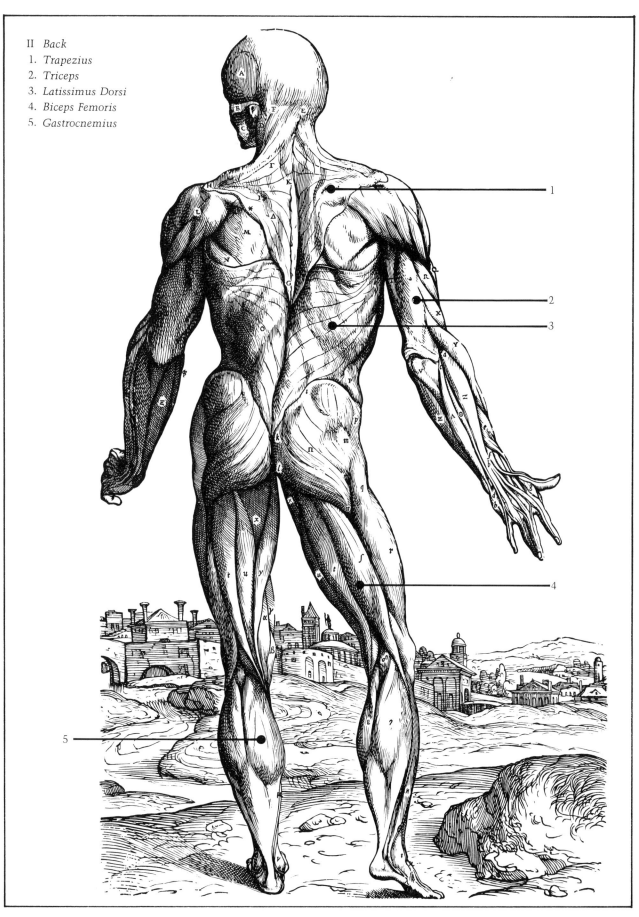

II *Back*
1. *Trapezius*
2. *Triceps*
3. *Latissimus Dorsi*
4. *Biceps Femoris*
5. *Gastrocnemius*

1

2

3

4

5

to 585 pounds, and not a lot of people need any more than that. There are a few at Gold's who do. For them there are one-hundred-pound plates.

There are also machines: custom made, many-stationed unit gyms like the Universals; lat machines; leg-press, hack-squat, leg-extension and cable-flye machines. There are even a couple of the relatively new Nautilus machines, chrome-and-Nauga-hyde contraptions that look like sophisticated torture devices. These are very chic machines right now. They are made by a man in Florida who claims they are revolutionizing bodybuilding. They are rarely used at Gold's. Most of the time they just sit there without the dignity of people in them, looking lonely and menacing.

If you happened to wander into Gold's off the street, and if you had never been in a bodybuilding gym before, it would seem as confusing as the inside of a clock—the oddly shaped metal everywhere, the cables and counterpoised masses of the machines, the mysterious-looking inclined benches and squat racks and sit-up tables. Right, you would tell yourself; but what is all this stuff supposed to do? If you had an uncommon eye for metaphor, you could maybe get an idea by looking up at the huge, intricate diagrams of railroad cars above the two long walls of mirrors. It is the simple function of those confusing pictures to clarify the internal structure of large things. So it is with the sprawl of equipment here. On any given morning during the summer you would find a group of very big men using that equipment loudly to clarify their bodies for competition.

Training is what they call it, and the way they do it here is so arresting that even if you were a person who does not care very much about bodies or about the people who do, if you had any kind of eye at all you would probably decide to hang around until it was over.

An old guy I knew in Iowa used to say that the only two parts of himself that interested him were his hands and one other part, and that his hands were only good for getting that other part out of his britches. Bodybuilders are less basic. They divide themselves up into six areas, or muscle groups: the back, the shoulders, the chest, the arms, the legs and the stomach. For a builder to do anything in competition, no one of these areas can be significantly less developed than the others, so a good bit of attention goes into balancing the training of all. The training of a muscle consists of first tearing it down with concentrated exercise, then allowing it to rest so that the tissue grows back a little larger than it was before. Because it is necessary for a muscle to rest while it grows and because of the importance of balanced development, most competitive bodybuilders train

Bob Birdsong

39

Ken Waller doing dumbbell benchpresses

Donkey calf-raises

on a split routine: they work certain parts of the body one day and rest those muscles the next while they work the others, alternating like that six days a week.

There are many different ways to split a schedule. Ed Corney, for instance, who trains up in Fremont, likes to work his stomach, shoulders and back together and to do an hour and a half of his workout in the morning and the other hour and a half in the afternoon. Here at Gold's, on Monday, Wednesday and Friday they train the chest, the back and the calves in the morning, and the upper legs and the stomach in the afternoons. On Tuesday, Thursday and Saturday they do shoulders, arms and calves in the morning and use the afternoons for tanning.

This is a Monday morning, around 9 A.M. A few people like Dave Draper who train early have already showered and gone. Franco Columbu, who starts at eight and likes to work out alone, is already into his lats. In the back there are four or five guys joking around, warming up while they talk. None of them lives here in California. Kent Kuehn and Denny Gable are from the South and Midwest. Bill Grant and Russell Long are from cities back East. And Pierre Vandensteen is from Belgium. Like the others he is here because this is training season, because this is Gold's, and because of the Austrian who is just now parking his silver BMW Bavaria in the lot outside.

Ken Waller stands behind the protein bar with a towel around his neck, thumbing a magazine. Before Waller got into bodybuilding he played pro football in the Canadian League; now he manages Gold's. He has red hair, freckles and a tough, country face. He is the only one who doesn't look up when Schwarzenegger swaggers in and throws a towel at the boys warming up in the back, a couple of whom have been waiting on him for fifteen minutes. "Come *on,* you guys," Arnold tells them. "I'm tired of waiting for you guys. Let's get *going.*"

Where he and Gable and Kuehn go, as soon as Arnold changes, is across the room to a foot-and-a-half-by-five-foot Naugahyde-covered, metal-braced bench to begin work on their chests—on the pectoralis muscles, called pecs, that lie between the collarbones and the rib cage. More than the arms, more even than the back, the chest is the seat of upper body strength. It is the bear's muscle—whose main and converse functions are to push things away from the body and hug things to it—and when developed properly it is very beautiful: two clean downward sweeps from the windpipe to the armpits and then an open flaring into the shoulders that give the body ovalness and depth above the waist. For some reason, maybe because they lie so close to vital organs, or because of the warm, dense, quick pump they take, the pecs are probably the most satisfying part of the body to work. And the primary exercise used to work them, the benchpress, is one of the most satisfying of all exercises.

"Like one time I was on the beach here and a girl was with a guy. She says to him, 'Look. This body. What a nice body this man has.' I says, 'Thank you very much.' And the guy says, 'Ahhhh. It's just weak. Weak muscles.' I went to him and I say, 'Why you say that?' I say, 'I'm stronger than you. I can show it to you. I can lift something and show you I'm much stronger than you. And I can also do athletic stuff. But you can't do it.' I said, 'Let's go to the platform, I'll show you.' And then he started getting upset. He says, 'Yeah?,' he says, 'I'll beat the shit out of you.' He said it. So I grabbed him by the neck. I said, 'Listen. Never say this again in your life.' So then his girl friend says, 'Okay. Okay. Now you can leave him alone.'"
—Franco Columbu

Schwarzenegger lies flat on the bench. At its head, behind his shoulders, are two pronged vertical arms that hold the Olympic bar a few feet above his face. Planting his feet wide on either side of the bench, he works his hands on the knurled bar for the place where it feels right, where it will ride evenly across the middle of his palms. Then he pops the bar off the prongs. As he lets the weight down he inhales to fill his lungs for pushing. The bar falls, touches his chest just above the nipples and rises, he exhaling with it, so smoothly that the motion looks pneumatic —seems to happen in a lubricated sleeve. Twelve times he lets the weight down and pushes it up, the pecs spreading to the fall and bunching to the rise like fists opening and closing. Each lift is called a repetition, or rep; twelve of them are a set. He and the other two men will do nine sets apiece, increasing the weight as they can for the first four and decreasing it as they must to get twelve reps for the last five. There is no waiting between sets, and no one is off the bench for more than a couple of minutes at a time.

This kind of competition training is known as bombing. It is a savage combination of the slow, heavyweight sets normally done to develop size and the quick high-rep work with lighter weights that develops definition and muscular clarity. In its energy and speed it is very exciting to watch, and murderous to do. Almost immediately the chest begins to hurt—a steady burning at first that turns into a deep raw ache of tissue and grows, so that the hardest sets are done through the most pain.

After the second or third set a rhythm develops. They are on and off the bench in smooth, quick rotation. The breathing is heavier and deeper. They talk the weight up for each other: "Keep it tight. . . . *Push* it now"—the mean-looking steel bar dropping and rising in a slight convex curve from the plates stacked at its ends. All of it—the sweating and concentration and noise—builds and synchs in around the central experience of the exercise: the flow of richly oxygenated blood to the muscle, the flush and tightening of skin as the tissue feeds and swells, coming up warm and heavy-feeling as though the work and pain, or even some of the iron itself, had been shoved in under the skin.

This is called a pump. It is the workout gone inside: the exercise swallowed and digested, metabolizing visibly into growth. Some bodybuilders will tell you that it feels better than coming. Whether that is true or not, it is one of the finest and most complicated physical sensations you can have. The part of the body being pumped feels like one of those fast-frame films of flowers blooming or seeds ripening; the muscles seem actually to go from pod to blossom in seconds under the skin.

A pump also makes you feel giddy and happy in the head, and as Schwarzenegger, Kuehn and Gable feel it coming up and

Bill Grant checking his stomach

Denny Gable

Leg presses

watch it in the mirrors, they begin to grin like Punky Stewart. Between sets they poke at their chests and stretch them out to feel the pump as far down as it goes. There are at least a half-dozen people around who are also pumped by now, and a general intaking exuberance, pleasuring and rowdy as a good party, spreads through the gym.

There are two kinds of exercises in a bodybuilding routine: the ones that build mass, or bulk as builders call it, like bench-presses for the chest, or squats for the upper legs, or bent-over rows for the back; and the ones whose function is to clarify the bulk—to carve and shape it the way you whittle a block of wood. The magical notion at the heart of the sport is that the body itself is an art medium: malleable, capable of being aesthetically dominated and formed the way clay is by a potter. A bodybuilder in training is a kind of sculptor of himself—the parent of a design of his body which he puts into competition with other designs. The traditional way of practicing the art is to bulk up with heavy weights and all the food you can eat, gaining twenty or thirty pounds of fat and muscle beyond where you want to be for competition, and then in the last month to go on a protein diet and chisel away all the fat with high-speed clarifying exercises, leaving only muscle. Bodybuilders call the last part of this process razoring, or cutting up, or ripping. They are all accurate words. But most of the best modern bodybuilders don't bulk and cut like that anymore. They work out fast with heavy weight, keeping themselves close to the skin. They bomb all the time, combining in their routines some exercises for bulk and some for cuts, and they hardly ever have a lot of fat to lose.

After the benchpresses, Schwarzenegger and his training partners do five sets of barbell presses on an inclined or slanted bench. This exercise concentrates and peaks the movement at the top of the chest and carves out the fine lateral striations on either side of the sternum. More than any of the other chest exercises, it hurts. They do five sets of twelve reps, hurting—Arnold more than the other two, because he does the exercise with greater purity. By the third set the enormous biceps that are his most incredible muscles—like two grapefruit on greased tracks inside his arms—have begun to quiver, and his upper chest is red and painful-looking as a cyst. One reason why Schwarzenegger is the best bodybuilder alive is that he never cheats an exercise. He makes every movement full and clean without jerking or pausing and without borrowing from muscles other than the one he is working. Another reason is that he concentrates so well.

Concentration in bodybuilding means thinking a muscle through what it is doing—forcing it with your mind, and with your eyes if you can stare at it, to work fully. As an ability, par-

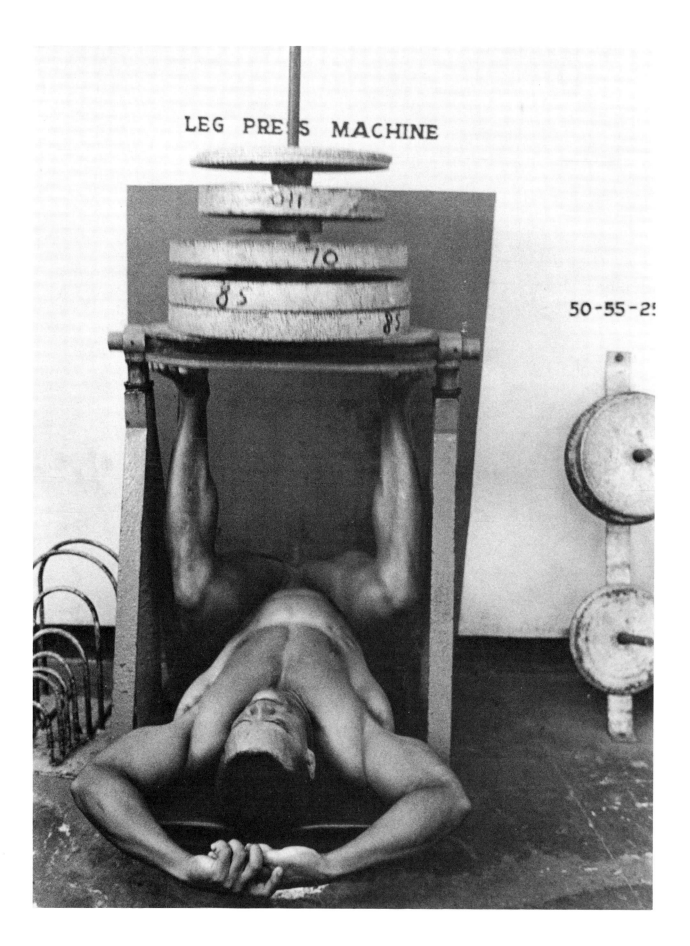

LEG PRESS MACHINE

50-55-25

ticularly in the definition exercises, it is one of the great sheep and goat separators of the sport. The people who cannot manage it very well tend to stay smooth. And all the best bodybuilders can block out an air war with their concentration. I remember watching Ed Corney doing dumbbell curls in Baghdad. He was seated on a stool in the middle of the big, strange gym that the city let the Mr. Universe competitors work out in. There must have been thirty or forty Iraqis standing along all four walls, and another fifty or so at the windows looking in. Ed Corney sat in the middle of all those fervid, noisy little people, staring at the sheath of his bicep fill and empty, fill and empty, his face remote and rapt as a Yogi's, his mind somewhere down inside the fibers of that arm.

After the inclined presses come five sets of dumbbell flyes and, finally, two sets of cable flyes. Both these exercises are designed to work the outside curves of the pectorals and their tie-ins with the deltoid muscles of the shoulders. Dumbbell flyes are done lying on a flat bench. The two weights are held over the chest and brought slowly down and out away from the body until the elbows are below the plane of the bench and the pecs are stretched back and out as far as they will go. Then the arms are pulled back upward in a curve toward each other—"Like you are hugging your girl," Arnold puts it—but only three-fourths of the way up, so that tension is kept on the muscles. For cable flyes, you stand and pull the handles of two weighted, pulleyed cables from above the head and beyond the shoulders, down across the body to meet in front of the crotch.

When they have finished with these exercises, Schwarzenegger, Kuehn and Gable will have made their chest muscles push or pull against metal a total of 278 times. Then they will go to work on their backs.

Across the gym, Franco Columbu is just finishing up on his, looking very professional as he always does when he is working out. He moves around the room from set to set with the aplomb and economy of an operating surgeon. Like Schwarzenegger, Franco is a natural athlete. At various times he has been a race car driver, an equestrian, a soccer player, a powerlifter and an amateur boxing champion of Italy. He has great charm and physical presence, and a highly developed sense of himself. You do not have to be told that Franco is very good at what he does. As with Arnold, there is an unmistakable aristocratic sheen, a polish of quality, on everything about him. He believes he will win the Olympia contest this year, and with good reason. He is as muscular as his small frame will allow, yet symmetrical and delicately carved. Except for his height he might have beaten Arnold before. He believes he can beat him this year despite it.

To start his back routine he did six or seven sets of wide-

Leg routine

grip, behind-the-neck chins, wearing a dumbbell on a strap around his hips to make them harder. Then rows, bending at the waist so that his upper body was parallel to the floor, and pulling up a barbell fifteen times to touch his abdomen. And then more rows, this time with a bar that has one end fixed to the floor and the other weighted with plates, crouching over the weighted end and pulling it to his chest. (Franco can do twenty-five repetitions of this exercise with three hundred pounds on the bar —a fact that doesn't really impress until you try one with that weight.) For his last exercise he is seated, facing a cable machine with his feet braced in front of him. Slowly, with as much stretch as he can manage, he draws two handles, connected by cable and pulley to two hundred pounds, from his feet to his upper abdomen and lets them back again. The muscles doing the work fan out on either side of his rib cage like wings.

Latissimus dorsi: they are called lats. They originate from the lower six thoracic vertebrae, the lumbar and sacral vertebrae (by means of the lumbardorsal fascia) and the crest of the ilium, and attach at their widest points to the humerus bones of the arm. Their functions are to rotate the arms medially and to draw the shoulders downward and backward. What all that physiological talk doesn't tell you is that the lats are the muscles you would use to lift a tree off someone. Nor does it tell you what glamorous and cocky things they are. Seen from the front of the body they flare out behind the chest in a wide V from the waistline to the upper arms, giving width to the torso and a curved depth of field to the rounded, ornate muscles of the chest and stomach. From the rear they are thicker-looking, and hump out from the spine like two legs of mutton to form an elegantly simple base for the convoluted smaller muscles in the upper back and shoulders. When they are developed, and particularly when they are pumped, the lats hold the arms out a little from the body, forcing the elbows wider than the shoulders. This way of standing or walking is the most identifiable physical characteristic of bodybuilders. It is their trademark, like a wrestler's neck.

The trapezius, rhomboideus, infra-spinatus, teres and levator scapulae are small, fancifully curved muscles lying near the lats that look in a good back pose as if they might have been shaped with different cookie cutters. When they are pumped, they bunch and tighten into a comfortable back-straightening countertension with the swell of the lats. And when that feeling is added to a chest pump, as it is in Franco right now, the whole upper torso feels dense and coiled and powerful as baled wire. It is a wonderful sensation, all that tightness—so satisfying and right that you are sure while you have it that it is the way a man's chest and back are supposed to feel all the time.

Franco does his last set of pulley rows feeling like that, en-

joying them one at a time, stretching each one out to pull down deeply into the muscles. Two or three weeks from now on a stage in New York he will want every line and cut he can bring up now, and knowing that makes the exercise even more enjoyable. Working out is always fun for him, but it is most fun in these last weeks before the contests when the training has to be flat out, and when everybody is around and into it together, creating a sense of shared momentum and priority. In the gym and on the beaches and in the health-food restaurants, there are people around now who haven't been around since this time last year —from New York, all over—everybody bombing and catching rays and razoring off: Franco and Arnold for the Olympia; Waller and Grant and Maldonado for the World; Kuehn, Birdson, Jeff Smith, Leon and others for the Mr. America. For all of them this time of year out here is a rite, a festival of eating and tanning and training that is done together to finish themselves into contest shape. It is also a time of self-criticism and revision, when they demand and get the most from themselves. That is really what Franco likes most about it. This is his time of year.

Kent Kuehn is sitting on a bench watching Bill Grant stand up on his tiptoes and then drop back flatfooted—up down, up down, like that on a machine, pushing up around three hundred pounds each time on his shoulders. Kuehn, Gable and Arnold have finished their backs and are into the fourteen sets of calf raises they do to polish off a Monday morning.

"Come over here and get a picture of Grant's calves before they disappear," Kuehn tells George Butler. "You'd never know this man spent three years in a wheelchair. Hey, Bill . . . Bill," he says to Grant, who is grunting out his last five reps, "what I want to know is how in the hell those little suckers can *burn* that much."

Grant is not amused. He has worked the muscles in question until they felt like they were going to explode, and still they won't come up right for him. Finished with the set, he looks wistfully over to where the best calves in the business are now busy doing donkey raises—pushing up two men astride Arnold Schwarzenegger's vast, horizontal back. The inner and outer gastrocnemius muscles in each of Arnold's calves swell out and downward from the back of the knee, meeting in a cloven bulge like an upside-down heart. They are satyr calves: flamboyant, breathtakingly tooled shapes that up until a couple of years ago were his poorest muscles—a body part he consistently gave away in competitions against Sergio Oliva, the great black Cuban builder from Chicago, who was then, as he is now, Arnold's only real competition.

Arnold decided they had to be bigger, better-shaped and lower on his shins. He made them that way by lifting weight and people with them over fifteen hundred times a week. And,

Dumbbell flyes

"You don't really see a muscle as a part of you, in a way. You see it as a thing. You look at it as a thing and you say well this thing has to be built a little longer, the bicep has to be longer; or the tricep has to be thicker here in the elbow area. And you look at it and it doesn't even seem to belong to you. Like a sculpture. Then after looking at it a sculptor goes in with this thing and works a little bit, and you do maybe then some extra forced reps to get this lower part out. You form it. Just like sculpture.

——Arnold Schwarzenegger

The calf

more crucially, by mentally forcing them to conform with what he thought they ought to look like. Even for him the body is a reluctant medium. It resists final forms with a vengeance, and to snap that resistance, to develop a calf or any other part of the body into what it is capable of being, requires hundreds of hours of demanding more than it wants to give—of pushing not only against the inanimate weight but with the mind against the organic recalcitrance of tissue.

By eleven-thirty all the people who started training around nine are finished. The calf workout ends, and the morning is abruptly over and silent. If you have been watching, Gold's feels suddenly like an auditorium or theater when a long applause stops all at once.

Franco showers quickly and leaves for a steak, green vegetables, yogurt and wine at his chiropractor fiancée's house.

Arnold will crowd his girl friend and a party of guys from the gym into his BMW and drive to some place like the Brownbagger—where, wearing emerald-green shorts and a T-shirt, looking as fancy and outrageous as a unicorn, he will cruise ahead of everybody else across a patio of small people eating spinach salads, and through the crowded main room to his table, where he will order a side dish of four scrambled eggs with his Stuffed Sirloin Spectacular, and tell a snowed and gaping hippy waitress that he doesn't vont the bread because it's not on his special sex diet.

And this afternoon between four-thirty and six, after lunch and a couple of hours on the beach, he will be back here with Franco and Kuehn and Gable and the others to work his stomach and his upper legs—doing dozens of sets of squats, front squats, hack squats and extensions for the long ellipsoid muscles of the frontal thigh, and leg curls for the biceps femoris muscles that run from his butt to the rear of his knees.

But before he does all that, and before he showers, he walks over to one of the big mirrors and takes off his shirt. The gym goes even quieter than it was before, and everyone still in it stops whatever he is doing. Looking thoughtful, Arnold turns his right calf forward and flexes it, watching in the mirror as the cleft muscle leaps into complicated relief. He twists it; studies it. Then he does the same thing with his left calf. Then he jerks both arms straight out in front of him and flexes his chest, and the motion seems to throw a fine sharp spray of excitement around the room. The men standing behind him watch the mirror in the same elated, adrenalized way you watch a fight as Arnold checks himself through five or six quick poses, his face now grinning and appraising wolfishly. They are all bodybuilders, a few of them very good ones, and they have all seen Arnold pose before, yet they stare at the reflection like the ladies on Santa Monica Beach when they see a builder for the first time.

Menu

It's not just his size that does this to people. There are a number of bodybuilders around who are as big, and a couple who are bigger. More than that, it is the perfect balance of everything —of biceps to calves, shoulders to waist, thighs to chest—and the detail and clarity of every part. Another thing is the naturalness and grace of his body. Most of the other very big builders, like young Lou Ferrigno, who has the greatest size ever but no polish, yet, look as if they have been built up with a trowel: the muscles look stuffed and worried into place. But each of Arnold's body parts, though huge, is subtly refined—as sleek and graceful-looking as the hind leg of a thoroughbred racehorse.

This quality is known as finish. It is the ultimate achievement for a bodybuilder, and it is very difficult to get. Of the men in Gold's Gym now only Pierre Vandensteen, the little Belgian whose upper body looks carved out of ice, has it. But the rest can recognize it whenever it is put up in a mirror for them, and see in it what each of them is working toward—where, with luck, the sweat and pain and discipline of this morning and all the other training goes.

None of them moves until Schwarzenegger is finished checkposing the muscles he has worked. Nobody wants to. They all know they are somewhere special, doing something important. One person, if he is big enough, can give a place this feel.

Three
Mr. Universe No. 1

George Butler and I went up to see Mike Katz and Ed Corney around two o'clock on the afternoon of the Mr. Universe contest. They had a room together on the floor above ours in the Hotel Baghdad, and they were asleep in it, taking a nap between lunch and some last-minute sun on the hotel roof.

We woke them up. They were lying in the low twin beds that were more like raised pallets than beds, covered to the waists with striped wool blankets, and neither of them seemed very chipper. Because of the heat and the heavy food and all the strange sensations, it took everybody a long time to come awake in Iraq.

"What time is it?" Ed Corney wanted to know. When he heard it was two he groaned. "We got to get some sun," he told Katz. "Pop out of there, big fella."

Katz just lay on the little bed, his eyes blank and unfocused, as though he were listening to himself wake up. He was propped on a pillow at the headboard, the muscles of his upper body segmented and hard-seamed as the carapace of a lobster.

Despite the armor-plated look, and despite his enormous size and the fact that he was for four years an offensive guard for the New York Jets, Mike Katz is a vulnerable-looking man—particularly when he laughs, or when he has just been awakened. He has a solemn, angular face, the only part of him that looks undernourished. He believes it is an ugly face and that it has always held him back. But it isn't ugly—or vacant and mean, as it can seem at first. It is intelligent and, once you know what you are looking at, vulnerable, and a little awkward, like his movements. Mike learned how to hold his face and how to move

Ed Corney
1972–73 IFBB Mr. America, 1972–
73 IFBB Mr. Universe
40 years old
5'6½" tall
170 lbs.
48" chest
19" arms
29" waist
26" thighs
17" calves

as a cross-eyed fat kid who was picked on in Hartford, Connecticut. Now he is the favorite for the title of Mr. Universe at the 1972 IFBB World Body Championships in Baghdad, Iraq; he is also a teacher and only a dissertation away from a Ph.D.—but he still does those things the same way.

At thirty-nine Ed Corney is eleven years older than Mike Katz, and he does not look even a bit vulnerable. He looks cheerful and self-possessed, and gentle in the way genuinely tough men usually do. About a year after the time in Baghdad I was at a party in a New York restaurant with Ed when an uptown lady began to needle him. She was sitting next to him and was a little drunk and maybe didn't know how to talk decently to him, so she began calling him "Mister" Corney, and began needling him about what he does for a living. What he does is bounce—thoroughly, and as nicely as it makes any sense to do that job—at a nightclub called Mr. Magooz in San Jose, California. Ed listened to her say she had never known a bouncer before and what a charming thing that was to do, and answered her when she asked him what he thought about when he bounced, smiling at her and calling her ma'am, but not in the same way she was calling him mister. He had paid out of his own pocket to come to New York for a contest he had not won. He was only two months off a big knee operation, and six off a second divorce. He needed her kind of talk like another bad knee, but he could see that this lady smoked and drank too much and, in her small, sharp face, that she was a lot worse off than he was.

He was born and raised in Hawaii, and his own face is broad, vaguely Asian, and very expressive, especially when he is posing. He got into bodybuilding late and has had good luck with it, but a lot of bad luck in other parts of his life. One of the pieces of good luck was that he learned how to pose from Clancey Ross, and nobody now poses with more joy, triumph and beauty than Ed Corney does. He doesn't have Katz's education, but he is bright, and very articulate about things that are important to him. He doesn't talk at all about the things that aren't.

At the time, he was the IFBB Mr. America. He had won the title two months before in New York, and winning this one in Baghdad too would give him the America and the Universe, two of the three biggest amateur titles, in the same year—something very few builders have done. As an older small man in a time of enormous young ones, he wanted badly to do it; though nobody gave him much of a chance against Mike Katz, who is one of the biggest of the young ones. Ed was giving away over half a foot in height, seventy pounds, and ten inches in the chest. Also, Mike was coming in very cut up, in his best shape ever, and wanting the contest with a fury. He had placed an embarrassing third the year before in Paris when it was supposed to be his year. Now this was supposed to be his year.

Baghdad, Iraq

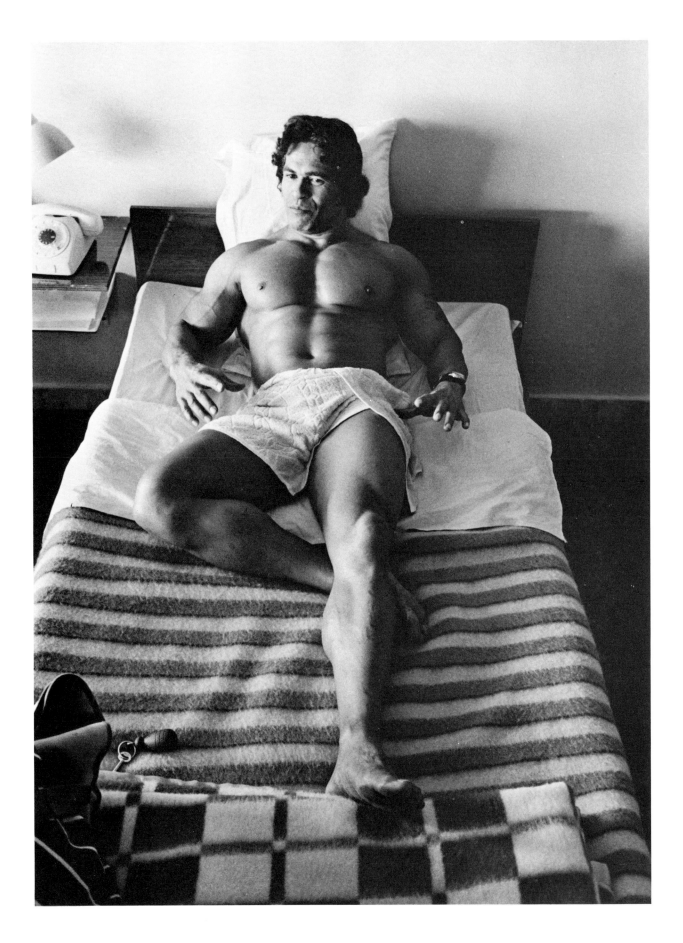

"You want a drink first?" Mike asked, finally coming to life.

"Sure," said Corney. He got up and wrapped a shabby hotel towel around his middle and went over to the basin that was in the room and washed his face, splashing water over his penny-colored chest and shoulders. "We've just got two hours. Weider says to be at the Cinema right at four. What's the story on using oil?"

"Can't use it," I told Ed. "The judges have declared it illegal."

Corney shrugged. His skin is naturally dark, with good bright tone. He would not miss using the baby oil in the contest as much as some. Like Katz, for instance, whose chalky skin needs the oil to bring out definition under the posing spot.

Mike grunted. He was set to anticipate that kind of news over here, a half-Jew in a crazy little Arab country where all his friends and his wife had told him he was nuts to come; he had been set ever since he got here for anything from having the oil banned on him to being sniped at from a roof, but so far the Iraqis had treated him with pure and simple idolatry, leaving him very little to grunt that way about. He got up to make one of the viscous protein drinks that he and Ed drank three times a day to ease their worries about the food.

Two and a half hours ago for lunch they had eaten a bowl of thin, unidentifiable soup, four well-done kebab patties made of ground meat and grain, and four eggs apiece. It *looked* safe, sure, and it tasted OK. But in bodybuilding, intake—the transference of liquids and solids to amino acids to proteins to muscle tissue—is half the ball game, and you don't take all that weird Arabic bread and dirty-looking fruit lightly. For lunch at home Mike would have had a pound and a half of lean ground round, cottage cheese, an apple or orange juice and a protein drink with eight ounces of milk, four eggs and six tablespoons of protein blended into it. That would make up about a third of the three to four hundred grams of protein he consumes every day, and make it up safely. But the only part of all that stuff you could bring with you to Baghdad was the protein powder.

He did have that. He opened his closet and looked at it, a huge can of Blair "Rheo-H" Protein Supplement, sitting on a shelf at the center of the other cans and bottles he and Corney had brought over with them. In addition to the protein, there were Weider Bone-Plus Vitamin D, Weider Super-B Concentrate, Weider 300-Milligram Vitamin C, Weider Brewer's Yeast and Iron, Weider Multi-Vitamin Mineral 100, Weider Supreme E Formula R_3, and a can of Blair "Rheo-H" Choline Plus, for the proper digestion of fat.

Mike took down the can of protein and carried it over to the basin. He pried off the top and took down the big blender cup they used for mixing.

They did have the powder, all right. But there was a story

Mike Katz
1971–72 IFBB Mr. America, 1972–73 IFBB Mr. World
29 years old
6'1" tall
240 lbs.
58" chest
21" arms
31" waist
29" thighs
18" calves

"You know my whole life seems —and I'm not feeling sorry for myself, but Nancy knows, she's been with me all my life—it always seems, I don't know whether it's because I've got a Jewish name or what it is, but it always seems like people have picked on me. You know—always trying to find fault with me. Constantly not giving me credit. Right from when I started playing peewee baseball, you know. I could throw a ball faster, I could run faster, I could do different things better, but I'd never start off—you know, play the whole game. And I always had that damn feeling as a youngster. You know I think sometimes that maybe why I'm doing what I'm doing is to get back at some . . . I don't know whether it's unconscious, but just to show the world, those people that made fun of me . . . and I was bullied quite a bit when I was a kid too, you know. It's a funny thing but I can remember and it sounds really weird: I had this bike. It was a real nice bike, you know. Kids are impressed with bikes when they're young—that's the big thing. And I can remember the fenders of the bike getting rusty. I never told anybody this. And I can remember the kids bothering me. Oh, man. Just bothering me about it. And another thing. I couldn't read that well, you know, and I had eye problems. And you know how kids can be really mean. My eyes sometimes crossed. I had two operations and the kids used to make fun of my eyes. And they used to make fun of the bumpers on my bicycle. Little

Baghdad airport

around that the water they had to mix it with might have, *could* have, in it these tiny little invisible snaillike things that could get into your bloodstream and. . . .

Things untellably strange and a certain amount of free-floating anxiety about them had been a part of this trip from the beginning. Bodybuilding contests themselves are exotic; but when you talk about pulling one together with contestants, delegates and press from thirty-two countries, and holding it in the city of Sheherazade, as the central event of five national days of banquets and bodybuilding-executive meetings and excursions to Babylon and down the Tigris River, and about preceding the whole deal with a thing called a Mr. Universe-in-Transit Ball in Geneva, Switzerland—you are talking then about something happening out on the farthest fringe of possibility.

Mike Katz is no dummy. He knows before most people do when things feel weird. He pointed to something printed in Arabic letters over the escape door in the big green-and-white Iraqi National Airlines chartered jet warming up to take us from Geneva to Baghdad by way of Athens—at least two of which places he had never either expected or wanted particularly to see.

"Do you guys know what that says?" he boomed to the planeload of French, Argentines, Belgians, Dutch, Welsh, Brazilians, Spanish, Finns, Canadians, Swedes, Americans, Swiss, and an eccentric Hawaiian named Dr. You who kept claiming loudly that he could create a world champion at anything within a week and that he had turned down five million dollars for the secret

Hotel Baghdad

of how to send a woman into space.

"What that says," Mike told them, only half joking, "is 'sucker' in Arabic."

The plane began to taxi. The pilot announced in English where we hoped to go and how long it would take, his voice vibrating like a sitar string in the high-pitched Middle Eastern accent that the whole world has come to associate with various kinds of airplane disasters. And all those huge men went quiet. They stopped talking the six or seven languages they had been talking and went suddenly big-eyed and pacific as children—over the Alps to Baghdad? in a green-and-white Iraqi plane with Arabic writing all over it, with a dude that sounds like *that* —more conscious than most, because of their size and strength, of gravity; and probably wanting more than most to arrive wherever the hell it was they were going, even if it was Oz, all of a piece, the parts still relating with some art to the whole.

And there was nothing about the way we were met at 2 A.M. at the airport in Baghdad to make Mike or anybody else feel any more at ease with things—greeted as we were by a cadre of small, swart, officious men in military uniforms and clipped mustaches, a few even with swagger sticks, who plied everyone with coffee, hurried their bags through customs, and created deferential little ceremonies for them all through the airport as though they were greeting a group of Russian economists instead of a planeful of bodybuilders.

That was the main thing out of joint, then and for the next four days. For Mike Katz and Ed Corney, and many of the other

things. And like there was a lady in school, she was a guidance teacher whose name was Mrs. Bassett. Nancy remembers. And she told me that I would never be able to become a college graduate, that it was impossible, that I just didn't have the intelligence and I should take up Industrial Arts. And man, you know from that peewee coach in baseball knocking me to the people in school. . . . I used to cry. In seventh grade I can remember the math teacher used to make fun of me and be sarcastic, and the reading teacher used to put me in the rottenest reading group. Man! You know those things I can remember as a kid did a helluva lot to make me push and show everybody what I could do. I think that's probably one of the, you know, had a lot to do with me wanting to achieve the greatness I want to achieve. Just to say, 'Hey, look at me now,' you know. 'You made fun of me then, but look what I turned into...' They used to call me Porky too. That was another thing they used to make fun of."
——Mike Katz

"Well, most people think that bodybuilders are strictly after their body in appearance only. I find that that isn't true. That's only half of it. The other half is it comes on rather strong in developing yourself mentally as well. A broad outlook on life— the trials and tribulations, ups and downs, you know. You're able to take things as they come and go."
——Ed Corney

In the Suk with Hussarian

builders, it was as if they had suddenly passed through a time warp—out of a place where they were unknown and snickered at, where their highest accomplishments were assumed to be deviant and freakish and where they had learned to live with all that, and into one where bodybuilding was the second most popular sport and where they were instantly recognizable heroes. Like Muhammad Ali or Hank Aaron. Even like Joe Namath.

"Meek Kitz?" said one little military man in an awed voice. He was beaming up at Mike, his wild Arab eyes spinning. "Ahhhhhg . . . Meek Kitz. Welcome, Meek Kitz, to *you and to all champions.*"

Katz stared hard at the man. Nothing in the other place had prepared him for this moment. But he *had* played on the same football team with Namath. And he did know to grab it while it was there. He could wonder about what it all meant later; worry then about whether or not there was anything sinister going on. So he smiled, with truly graceful largesse, and said, "Thank you. It's a pleasure to be here."

For the next two days he and Ed Corney went right on smiling like that through one indecipherable but pleasant situation after another: on the dusty streets where they were followed and beleaguered by hordes of men and children shoving papers at them to sign, the retinue growing as they walked, so that after four or five blocks there might be thirty people winding behind them through the strange streets that swarmed with robed men and veiled women, with bicycles, pushcarts and 1953 Chevrolets; or down the stone alleyways of the medieval *suk*s, the ancient

Supper with the Mayor of Baghdad

copper, silver and gold bazaars in Old Baghdad whose stunning Elizabethan raunchiness of crowded smells and noises, of texture laid on texture, of cramped, shrill ripeness bounded by treacherous shadows and decay, lay over and smeared all their perceptions like Vaseline on a camera lens.

And at lunch on Sunday, the day after we arrived, at the Al-Mansoon Racing Club with chief delegates from various national bodybuilding federations—strange-looking, bulky men in tight suits from places like Pakistan and Kuwait, Thailand and Turkey, many of them fingering worry beads. The club was an airy second-story room bordered by a terrace that overlooked an enormous beturbanned crowd, and beyond it to an emerald-green mile-and-a-half track where there were races going on. Vendors down below in the crowd sold slices of melon and cups of thick, bitter coffee. The jockeys rode magnificent Arabian horses and wore long bright silk plumes on their helmets that streaked behind them in races against the hot blue sky. Lunch was a mammoth buffet of whole twenty-pound fish, a side of lamb on a bed of yellow rice, chickens, the wheat circles full of meat called kibbie, sausages, beans with lamb, fruit cakes and custards. The Eastern delegates were the first at it, using their hands to tear off meat and serve their plates; and when everyone else was through, the servers and army drivers formed a line on either side of the table and savaged what was left, shoveling it into their mouths with both hands. Mike and Ed and the few other bodybuilders there ate as though they were picking lint off a lapel. They stood with their backs to walls, smiled steadily, and gazed out over the heads of the delegates at the bright races on the track.

Or at the prejudging for the short class which was held the next day on a lovely, cool, darkening late afternoon at El-Shaab Hall. After the posing, when everyone had looked over the small but very chiseled and worked Belgian, the big smooth South American with the heavy waist, and the nearly perfect Japanese and Egyptian who would take one and three in the class, they retired to an oval trellised garden outside the hall, bodybuilders and managers in sweat suits mingling and chatting quietly with the delegates and officials as if at tea on a Kensington lawn. At the center of the garden was a stone terrace. At the center of the terrace was a red inclined bench and three silver barbells; and somehow they looked perfectly natural out there, correct and dignified as a ship in a bottle at a yachting party. Ed Corney stood for a while at the edge of the terrace looking at the bench and the weights, dealing with them through the easy air as symbols, objects of respect—wagging his head and smiling.

And maybe especially at the dinner later that night given by the mayor of Baghdad for over three hundred people at Al-Zawrah Park. Held outside, under canopies and the stars, with illuminated pools between the buffet tables and fountains

"I want to be bigger than everybody else, but I wouldn't want to
be so big that people can't accept
it. For instance, if you come in
with 30-inch arms, even your
own peers aren't going to accept
that. I wouldn't want to be that
way. I wouldn't want to infinitely
become unreal."
——Mike Katz

An Iraqi gym

splashing and colored lights strung between poles—it was as festive and cordial as a Charleston debutante party. And Ed and Mike were there at the center of things, receiving compliments and eating carefully, shaking hands with endless foreign well-wishers, wondering at it all, and grinning their heads off.

Mike Katz stirred six tablespoons of protein powder into a full blender cup of the suspect water. He took some vitamin pills, chased them with half the mixture and gave the other half to Ed Corney. Then he took from a drawer *Le Maillot Culturiste* posing trunks he uses for contests, wrapped them carefully in a towel and stuck them in his gym bag for later.

"Let's get some sun," he said. "How much time we got?"

"Hour and a half until we have to be there. We can lie up there for an hour anyway," said Ed. "You guys coming up?" he asked me and George.

"How do you feel?" Mike asked him.

"Great. A little edgy. How about you?"

"Good," said Mike. "I feel good. But I wish it was over and we were back in the States. God, would I garbage up. What are you going to do over here? You gonna garbage up on those sheep's heads we saw boiling out in the street?"

Corney combed his black hair in the mirror and chuckled. They each had on workout trunks and sandals, and each of them had two towels to lie on up on the hot tile roof.

"You know they're televising this thing?" said Ed, putting down the comb. "It's going to be carried all over Iraq."

Mike Katz held the door open for him, smiling again, wide awake now, ready for anything. "Not just Iraq," he said. "They're showing it all over the Middle East."

Four

Serious training to a competitive bodybuilder means four things —exercising, eating, sleeping and tanning; and for as long as six months before a contest these four things are practically all he does. The last is separate from the others and important only to white builders; but as a way of giving the skin color and uniform finish under the lights, it is very important to them.

The other three are connected inside the body in a lovely mysterious machinery known as anabolism—the process by which simple substances are synthesized into the complex materials of living tissue. Anabolism is constructive metabolism, and "Metabolism" comes from the Greek word for change. Constructive change is what bodybuilding is all about. Simply put (because there is no better way to put it; like every process and fact of the human body it is beautiful and moving beyond language and can only be oversimplified as I am about to, or overcomplicated as physiologists do), it works like this: heavy, orchestrated exercise tears down the tissue of the muscles, and sleep and diet combine to replace and rebuild it, producing new and stronger flesh.

In any of the first-rate bodybuilders the three parts of this relationship are as finely adjusted, one to the others, as the mainsprings in a Piccard watch; and the result of that adjustment is a near-total control over the physical proportions—a protean capacity to manipulate weight and spaces by fractions of pounds or inches. That is a capacity unique in all the world to bodybuilders, as is the particular intimacy it gives them with their bodies.

Of the three, sleeping is the easiest to handle correctly. All you have to do is know exactly how much sleep is right for you

"Listen, I've been on countless TV shows, given countless lectures, and traveled all over the country for nothing, on behalf of youth groups and other organizations, just to try to change the image of what people thought a muscle man or bodybuilder was. But they all would say, 'Well, fine, great; there's ripples, there's lumps—that's, you know, what for?' A lot of people who have been honest with me have told me that there's an insecurity being around someone who's physically overpowering."
—Steve Michalik

Steve Michalik

71

and then manage to get it every day. I've known a few good builders who got by on four or five hours. Joe Disco sometimes went for weeks on that. Another one I know needs twelve. He swears that he can hear himself growing during the last three and that the sound is like Cornflakes being poured into a bowl. The exercising part is trickier. It takes a builder a long time to learn which ones are best for him, how best to mix and split them, when to increase or decrease weight and reps, and all the other thousand things he has to know to get the most from his workouts. But the hardest of the three to control with accuracy is eating. It is hardest because it allows the most room for mistakes and because of the truly bewildering variety of growth-producing foods, pills, powders, liquids and drugs that *can* be ingested.

The basics are simple enough: even a beginning bodybuilder knows to eat numerous small meals during a day instead of one or two big ones in order to avoid systemic and digestive overload —meals that are long on necessary vitamins, and protein foods like meat, cheese and eggs, and short on starches, fats and sugars. So he does that, and maybe takes a few supplemental vitamins, and drinks a protein drink at night made, maybe, out of Tiger's Milk, protein powder, peanut butter, two raw eggs and soybean oil, and he thinks he is doing everything right. But then some guy in the gym mentions that his tendons would be stronger if he ate a little kelp or dulse for the chlorine in it; or suggests he stop eating all that chard because too much sodium is building up his water table. Or he read that Franco Columbu takes vitamin E with vitamin A *before* meals, and B-complex with hydrochloric acid during them; or that Steve Michalik used to take two hundred desiccated liver tablets a day.

He hears about something called panothenic acid that he can find in crude molasses; and biotin, a dynamite vitamin in yeast. He learns about cold-pressed wheat germ oil for increasing stamina and reducing stretch marks; lecithin, for thinning cholesterol; predigested liquid proteins; shark liver oil; choline and inositol for getting rid of subcutaneous fat and bringing out cuts; nicotinic acid, for metabolizing the sugars he is not supposed to eat and preventing pellagra; and cobalamin, or vitamin B-12, which will help increase his appetite for all this stuff. By now he is long out of basics. Nothing is simple anymore.

He finds out quickly that it is not only confusing but expensive to eat the way he is supposed to, that he will have to spend enough on food—just plain *food*, let alone all the pills and powders and things—to support two or three ordinary people.

Take Steve Michalik, for instance. Michalik is a chatty, sensitive, self-conscious man with a quick mind, a feel for publicizing himself, and a kinky love-hate relationship with bodybuilding. He is coming back to competition now after a two-year retirement, but he despises the demands it makes on him and his wife—not least the fact that for a year before he won the 1972 AAU Mr. America title she had to eat every meal with her mother because Michalik's food alone was running them seventy dollars a week. To gas up his anabolism every morning he would eat for breakfast two cube steaks, a sixteen-ounce can of tuna fish, cottage cheese, three or four hard-boiled eggs and a quarter pound of yellow cheese, and follow all that with a protein drink. Then two hours later he would eat again: a whole chicken, water-soluble vegetables, four hard-boiled eggs, more cottage cheese. Another drink. Pills. He forced himself through six of these meals a day.

He was working then as a commercial artist in Manhattan and he was lucky enough to have a boss who was fascinated with the great sea changes going on in Michalik. The boss bought him a grill, a hotplate, a blender and a refrigerator to facilitate his eating at the office. He bought him a lounge chair to sleep in for two hours each day, and he did not mind the hours of work Steve missed because he was training. This made things easier, but no less expensive. Nobody knows better than Michalik the various costs and difficulties of becoming a Mr. America. He nearly went broke and almost lost his marriage while doing it. And nobody knows better than he how little that title is worth on the open market. But if you ask him about it today, now that he blames bodybuilding for ruining his life, he'll tell you he would have eaten grease out of a crankcase at a dollar an ounce to have won it.

There is a part of this intake aspect of bodybuilding training that is not only complex and expensive but controversial, murky, widely lied about, and used by a lot of people to criticize the sport. It is the use of various drugs, mostly synthetic hormones, and it is much more talked about than it is understood. There are stories around about builders snorting coke and dropping reds and Dexedrine for energy. Maybe some do; I've never seen it or heard about it from anyone who knew what he was talking about, and the same is true with the stories you hear about guys getting their calves or arms shot up with silicone in Mexico. If these things happen, they happen with a very small percentage of builders and with virtually none of the best ones. Some bodybuilders do try thyroid and pituitary shots for a while to step up their metabolisms, but most of them find that the shots don't really do that much and stop. But the drugs that draw the most attention and the most flak are the anabolic steroids, and there is no question that practically all first-class competitive bodybuilders do use or have used them.

Steroids are synthetic testosterone, a principal male hormone produced in the testes that affects secondary sex characteristics. They are used medically to treat protein depletions, arthritis,

"Then there's the off days. You're stuck with this off day, right? Well what are you going to do with the off day? Well I might as well do my calves. And I might as well do my waistline. I might as well do my forearms. I might as well do incidentals. I might as well work on definition. I might as well work on posing. You know, I might as well run to the library and learn more about what I should be eating at this particular time. Learn about metabolism, you know. And meanwhile while I'm doing this, there's my wife sitting home going bananas. And my mother, the clergy at the church and everyone saying, you know: 'What are you doing? Take a day off.' I say, okay, fine. Sundays I'm going to rest. Sundays I find myself doing one-legged calf-raises on a street corner somewhere. Because when I'm up on that stage, I'm there by myself. Me alone. I'm not up there with a baseball bat. I'm not up there with a football. I'm there with just me. My body."
—Steve Michalik

you've come a

Just a year or so ago champs had to get their food boosters from nutritional drinks made for the average guy . . . drinks weak in protein, vitamins and other elements needed to build muscle and power . . . drinks made with artificial ingredients — chemicals — cyclamates — and other additives.

But today — 1972 — they know better. They know there's a complete lineup of delicious, nutrition-packed Weider Wildcats made especially for them to help feed their muscles what they need for championship growth . . . a bomber's load of nutritional Wildcat power!

In '72 you have yo

powe

ong way champ!

These Powerizers are almost 'supernatural' the way they work. The champs know them as great nutritional boosters that help make musclebuilding come alive! And they know that the Powerizers do powerful things to their muscles . . . that you just can't beat the scientific blend of high-nutrition ingredients that is deliciously, uniquely Weider.

Some come on . . . put it all together in '72! Make your muscles come alive with this great lineup of nutritional Wildcat Powerizers made especially for the champs . . . made for **you! You've come a long way, champ!**

own 'breed' of Wildcats!

geriatric problems and anemia, and to help people recover from long sicknesses. They are also used to beef up cattle, and are known bleakly to give acne to women. The bodybuilders, weight lifters, wrestlers, football players, track men in the weight events, and other athletes who use them, do so because they believe they make them heavier and stronger. Whether or not they actually do is still in court. Of eleven recent controlled studies, six found that weight and strength are increased by the drugs, five found that they are not. The researcher in charge of the most recent of these studies is Dr. Larry Golding of Kent State University. Golding probably knows as much about the relation of steroids to sport as any man in the country, and it is his belief and the finding of his study that steroids cannot make anyone bigger or stronger except by a touching psychological mechanism known as the placebo effect—believing in the drug so strongly that belief produces the results that the drug is supposed to produce.

Regardless of what Dr. Golding and other scientists find in laboratories, most bodybuilders believe that they cannot build themselves beyond a certain point without steroids, and that to stay competitive they have to use them. But they don't like doing it (they usually deny that they do until you get to know them well, and are quick to point out that if steroids were all it took, any Jack on the street could make himself a Mr. Olympia with just a prescription), and they will stop on a dime or cut down, as Arnold Schwarzenegger did over a year ago, when they are convinced they can get along without them.

They don't like using them partly because it lays them and the sport open to the use-one-use-them-all criticism often insinuated by people who don't know any better, that bodybuilding is rife with junkies. And because of the unsubstantiated but ubiquitous rumors about how the drugs can ruin your liver or make you go bald, or even wither up your balls. But mostly they don't like using them because they sense that in an oblique way doing so gives some weight to one of the most abhorred of all the many public discomforts about them: that all those muscles somehow come out of a bottle; that there is something as synthetic, unhealthy, useless and faintly sinful as plastic flowers about what they do and the way they look—as though all the discipline, sacrifice and work of their training, and the organic balance of exercise, fueling and rest that has to be found and struck exactly right inside the body before the outside becomes a proper medium, and the sane, satisfying connection between the body's health and its beauty, and how good they feel all the time, how good the lungs feel, and the skin, and how they can almost hear the blood circulate, and how easily they can move themselves and other things—as though all those things counted for nothing, could be reduced to something the size of a pill.

Dr. Golding himself wondered. He had run physiological

tests on other athletes, regular *athletes*, at his applied-physiology research center in Kent, but never on one of these blown-up fellows. Did their training, he wondered, put them "in shape," or was all that muscle the result of some dark pill alchemy and as useless as so much cotton batting under the skin? So through Ben Weider, president of the International Federation of Bodybuilders, he got himself an invitation to Baghdad, where he met Mike Katz, and a month or two after the contest he had Katz come out to Kent State to undergo a battery of tests. He dunked Mike in tubs of water, took skin-fold and body measurements, had him ride a stationary bicycle, and counted his pulse over and over. What he found was that Katz was phenomenally fit: every one of his scores was in the superior rating except for his sitting heart rate, which was a high good; he was only eleven percent fat, five percent below normal, his subcutaneous fat was practically nonexistent, and his cardiovascular system and aerobic capacity were spectacular.

But the most telling fact was the result of the bicycle-ride test that measured Mike's physical-work capacity (PWC). What it told is all anybody needs to know about a world-class bodybuilder's training. The test determined that Mike's maximum work load was 2,400 KPM. That meant that his PWC was completely off the scale they used to measure it.

"I was interested in the beauty of the male physique, and showing the beauty of the male physique to whoever had paid to come to see it. So I would move to music, and pose, and do sort of ballet, and go down and twist and forward, just so it looked . . . it would look almost like if you looked at a lion running through the jungle. Sometimes if you can catch a lion, or a horse or a doe—they're so beautiful just the way they move. And I would try to incorporate this in my posing. Definitely not putting any real muscley, veiny type poses in there, because I didn't want to turn anyone off. I just wanted to bring the beauty of the male physique across. Because I really feel that the male physique is just as beautiful if not more beautiful than the female's. Now horses, the male is prettier. Male lion. The peacock. I love women and everything. But, well, look at me. I just feel that a man has as much to offer as a woman."
——Steve Michalik

Five
Mr. Universe No. 2

It was hot on the roof. The sky was the same parched blue it was every day from dawn to sunset—a dusty, deserty blue—and the sun lay across the width of it like varnish on a windowpane. Few of the noises drifting up from below sounded real. And whenever Mike Katz or Ed Corney stood up, wandered to the edge of the roof and looked out into the teeming streets, or over the random sprawl of blocky sand-colored buildings to minarets and palm trees on an aquamarine horizon, not much looked real either. It all seemed like—ahh, well, like a movie. Particularly since the whole city was so tuned in to them. It was almost as if all the noise and movement down there on the streets was *for* them in a funny way—as if they were the central characters in a fantasy, like kings of Mardi Gras.

Right at that moment, for instance, wasn't Hussarian, their assigned chauffeur, a shy, unctuous student of English from the University of Baghdad whose eyes could not have been directed by John Huston to spin with more awe whenever he looked at them—wasn't good old Hussarian just inside the roof door over there keeping back a ragged horde who would cheerfully have stood swaddled in bearskins on the steaming roof just to watch Meek Kitz and Et Carney catch a few rays? Who knew? It could have been thousands, half of Baghdad, that Hussarian was holding off—clutching a scimitar or something, his soft eyes gone hard with purpose.

As the afternoon wore on toward four, Ed Corney and Mike Katz flipped themselves over occasionally, sweated freely in private stews of images and nerves, and tried not to think about the contest. They had each dreamed the night before that the other

"Why does this particular thing turn people off? I believe that people should be built the way I'm built. I don't think people should walk around looking like a piece of junk. I've got normal clothes on—if they fit tight maybe it's because I can't afford clothes that don't fit tight. I don't have anything showing that shouldn't be showing. Some guys walk around really freaky, but that turns me off too. When I go to the beach I have these little areas where nobody goes but seagulls. Nobody bothers me. I want to compete—I want to be the greatest in the world. If that's wrong, it's wrong."
—Mike Katz

Mike Katz, hulking the lineup

"Sometimes when you're working out in the gym and you're so much more developed and, you know, unbelievable in comparison to anybody working out around you, you say to yourself, 'Man, am I real? Is it possible that I really am this big?' And sometimes, you know, I'll gander at the mirror when I'll see some little guy who's working pretty hard go by and I'll say, 'That's ridiculous; how can this be possible?' Then I start, sometimes I find myself looking for defects in the mirror, you know, to see if I'm really that big or if there may be a mistake—you know, a wave in the mirror that makes you look bigger. I don't get hung up thinking about it, but sometimes I do. You know you're not normal, because normal is 6 feet tall, 150 or 160 pounds, you know, fairly skinny; or a big fat person. So that you know that because you're superiorly built, and you've trained and developed that way, that you do look odd. I mean, you do look unreal."
—Mike Katz

The Palestinian team

one would win the Mr. Universe title. If there was ever a place that seemed right for taking omens seriously, this place had to be it, and neither one of them liked his dream very much. Also, they had seen each other pose that morning at the prejudging for their height classes and determined privately, as everybody else had, that the overall title had to go to one of them; but also that it could go to *either* one.

Mike had had no serious competition in the tall class. He looked very confident in the lineup, vastly bigger than anyone else and even more cut up than he had been in New York a couple of months before when he beat Ken Waller for the Mr. World. There was a heavily muscled Iraqi with less calf even than Mike in the line, and a smooth symmetrical Spaniard named Baldo Lois; but the rest of the class was like the two doe-eyed Palestinians who looked like brothers and went everywhere together holding hands—serious but hopeless, five or six light-years away from Mike Katz. Mike had hulked them bad in the lineup—wearing himself like armor, waiting until they were already into their poses before he hit his, and making sure all of them saw that if he decided to spread his lats, he could hide any two of them. Corney's class, the mediums, had been better. A Swede, a Frenchman, a Belgian and the Iraqi had all looked good, and any one of them could have won the class if he had not had the bad luck of having Ed Corney in it with him. Relaxed, inside himself, staring as he always does at a point on the back wall of the gallery, he had a tight density of presence in the line that made him seem the only one in it. And he posed flawlessly, flowing purely as water from shot to shot in that quietly dramatic way of his that emphasizes the perfect balance and clarity of his muscles—not knocking people over with his size the way Katz does, not even flexing, really, so much as arranging the muscle groups in smooth serpentine shifts that surprise and gratify as you watch. It is a balletic kind of posing that no one does as well as he. Frank Zane, another major bodybuilder with a similar style, makes it look too soft and choreographed; with Corney every movement is virile, spontaneous and pure.

By the end of the morning both of them knew that they would win their classes, all right; and that they had only each other to worry about for the title. But after watching each other pose, that had seemed like more than enough.

Around three-thirty they left the heat and images on the roof and went back to their room to get ready. Hussarian came along.

"Iss time to go," he suggested as soon as Ed had shut the door.

"Relax," Mike told him. Which was exactly what he and Ed then proceeded to do. Back in the room with familiar rituals to perform, nothing weird to look at or hear, and with the contest too close to think about, both of them nerved out, went calm, and began enjoying themselves.

Prejudging

"He [Ed Corney] has a slightly
more finished physique than I
do. He's a little rounder. You
know, he's got no weak points
and my arms could be slightly
bigger. My calves could be bigger.
And his physique—he's not over-
whelming; he's not huge or dynamic as far as his physique
goes. But he's just very symmetrical. You look to try to find flaws
in him and there's just very, very
little you can find."
——Mike Katz

Talking and clowning, Mike stood in front of a mirror and gave his arms, legs and chest a quick final shave with an injector razor. Then he covered them with a light coat of Tan-in-a-Minute, feathering the stuff out with his palms so it would leave no lines, and got Ed to rub some of it into his back. After the lotion had dried he rubbed a thin, expert film of baby oil over it, and then checked himself over in the mirror, looking very carefully at his red-bronze, glinting surface.

Hussarian had watched all this with a vague, stoned expression on his face like a baby watching fire, and it wasn't until Mike was completely finished with himself and dressing that he returned enough to notice that the contest was due to start in five minutes. "Sheee*eet*," he said simply.

"Whassat, Hussarian, old buddy?" asked Ed, who had dressed quickly in jeans and a wild blue-and-white Hawaiian shirt and had been ready for minutes. He knew we were all going to be late but hadn't mentioned it because the last twenty minutes had been fun, and most of all loose, and there wasn't a lot of that around this place. "What's eating you?"

"We go now," said Hussarian, scuttling over to Katz. "Eeeeeii . . . *we go now quickly, Meek Kitz*," he pleaded.

Katz looked at him, then at Corney, then at me, his lean face serious and quizzical. He had just been combing his hair, for God's sake. Now what was this little-mother *act?*

"We're running a little short on time," Ed told him. "Hussarian's worried about it. Why don't you ask him can he whip out a flying carpet?"

The suggestion didn't even sound facetious. I mean for kings of Mardi Gras? Why the hell not?

Ben Weider was more than just mad; he was pale around the lips and quivering when the American team arrived at the Al-Nasr Cinema twenty minutes late.

"You have *missed*," he told them, "the international march. There was no one to carry in the American flag."

We had come in through the backstage door of the Cinema, which houses the largest auditorium in the Middle East, and the corridors were a bedlam of rocketing Arabs, photographers, half-dressed contestants, and people with IFBB badges trying to tell everyone else what to do. Beyond the stage over two thousand people were packed into the seats and standing spaces of the auditorium, and there were at least another thousand outside milling, making mad rushes at the door, and reaching plaintively through the bars on the building's windows, only to have their arms rapped methodically by the billies of officials standing inside. With all the noise and confusion, and with at least a half-dozen pairs of small dark hands clutching at each of them, it was very difficult for Ed and Mike to pay attention, even to the

Mr. Sweden, Mr. France, Mr. America

Oiling up

enraged president of the International Federation of Body-builders.

"What?" one of them asked him.

"You are *late*, you are very, very horribly *late*. The international march is over and the short class is already on stage. *Where have you been?*"

"We were dressing," Ed told him. "Where do we change?"

Just then a frantic-looking Iraqi official came tearing around a corner wringing his hands and crying hysterically at the backs of two South American builders, "No*aisllle*, no*aisllle*, no*aisllle*..."

It was a horrible, keening statement that might have been announcing rape, fire—any one of a dozen disasters. And like the dreams, and the being late, it was mighty like an omen. Whatever it was, it stunned the backstage into near silence.

"What's he saying?" asked Mike Katz. "This place has gone *crazy*."

As Ben Weider began to hustle him and Ed through the crowd to the dressing room, both hands full of their triceps, Hussarian sidled up to Mike.

"He say no *aisle*." Hussarian rubbed his chest. "It iss not allowed for champions to use aisle on the body."

"Oh," said Mike. "Oh, yeah." But he wasn't really listening anymore. He was finally getting ready to do what he came here to do, what he had waited and trained for a year to do. And he didn't care if everybody else in this fantasy went stark raving crazy.

Serge Nubret at the Lion of Babylon

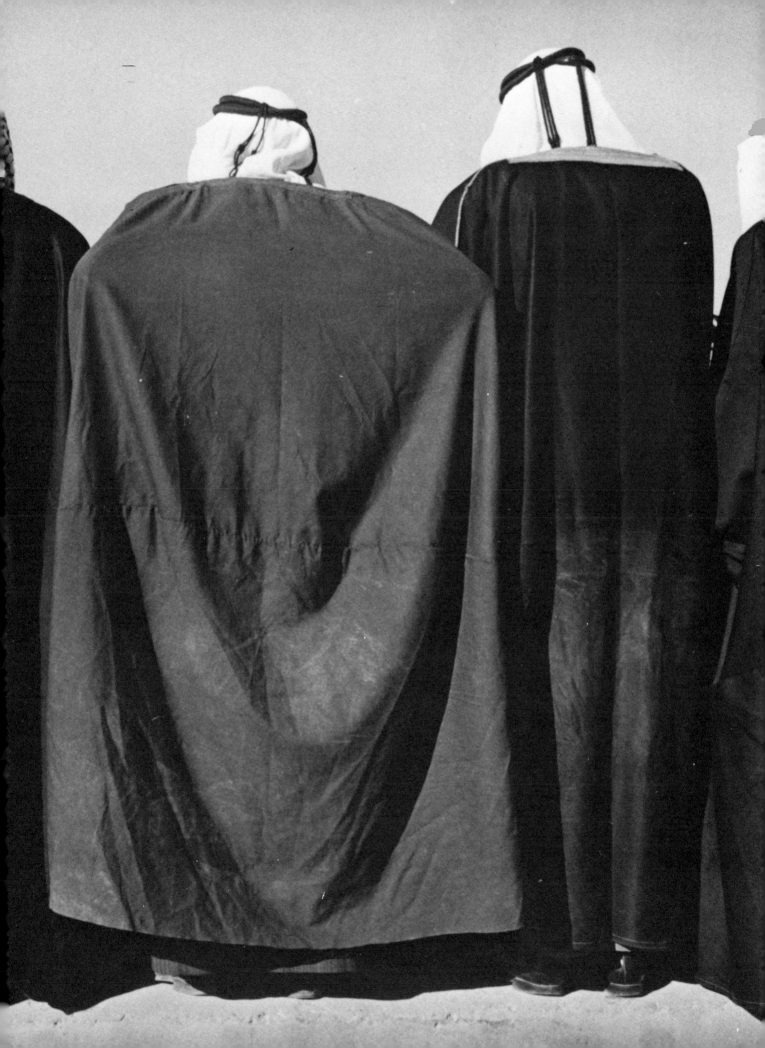

Six
Mr. Olympia No. 2

Over in the sandy general-exercise area there are men and women climbing ropes and working out on balance beams and parallel bars. Pickup games of basketball, volleyball and soccer are going on, and from where the beach begins to the loud dirty Pacific fifty yards away, as far as you can see in either direction, is knee deep with people. Stationed along the bicycle path above the beach are delicate little concrete tables, and at one of them a Saturday luncheon party of winos dreams out over all of this, taking the sun.

Between the paddle-tennis courts and the basketball is the weight-lifting platform and beside it a bright green sward of grass with a lot of big men in small bathing suits lying around. This is bodybuilders' turf: their piece of Venice Beach, as separate from the rest of it as Gold's Gym is. It is around two o'clock on Monday, the outside, digestive part of the day between morning and afternoon workouts. There are a few middle-aged builders out, old-timers from the days of Muscle Beach, with their young wives and babies and small waists. A couple of girl friends. A doctor who specializes in nutrition. A powerlifter in a wheelchair with enormous arms and no legs. And a girl bodybuilder with a big dog named Oberline. The rest are guys from Gold's who are getting ready for New York and to whom this tanning is serious business, almost as important a part of their day as training or eating. All of them but one lie as stiff as corpses, moving only to turn.

The other one is Arnold Schwarzenegger. He sits at the center of things in a bright-orange brief, shades, and a borrowed wide-

"There are some girls who are turned on by my body, and some others who are turned off. But for the majority I just use it as a conversation piece. Like someone walking a cheetah down 42nd Street would have a natural conversation piece. Then when they get to talking to me they see I am not mean but gentle to them and that's all they want to know."
—Arnold Schwarzenegger

Bodybuilders' turf, Venice Beach, Calif.

"When a homosexual looks at a bodybuilder, I don't have anything against that. I would probably stare the same way if Raquel Welch or Brigitte Bardot walked by. If I see a girl with big tits, I'm going to stare and stare. And I'm going to think in my mind what I'm going to do with her if I would have her. The same is true with the homosexual—he's looking at the bodybuilder and picturing what he would do with him. You have to face it if you have a good body, and it is somehow a compliment to a bodybuilder. Sometimes girls are attracted to your body; sometimes homosexuals are attracted to your body."
——Arnold Schwarzenegger

"I have a good sense of my body in a bathing suit around people who appreciate what I'm doing, like a contest. Then I'm proud. On television I am proud. But on a beach most people are not experts. The general public doesn't know how to look. How proud can you be when they don't even know what they're looking at?"
— Arnold Schwarzenegger

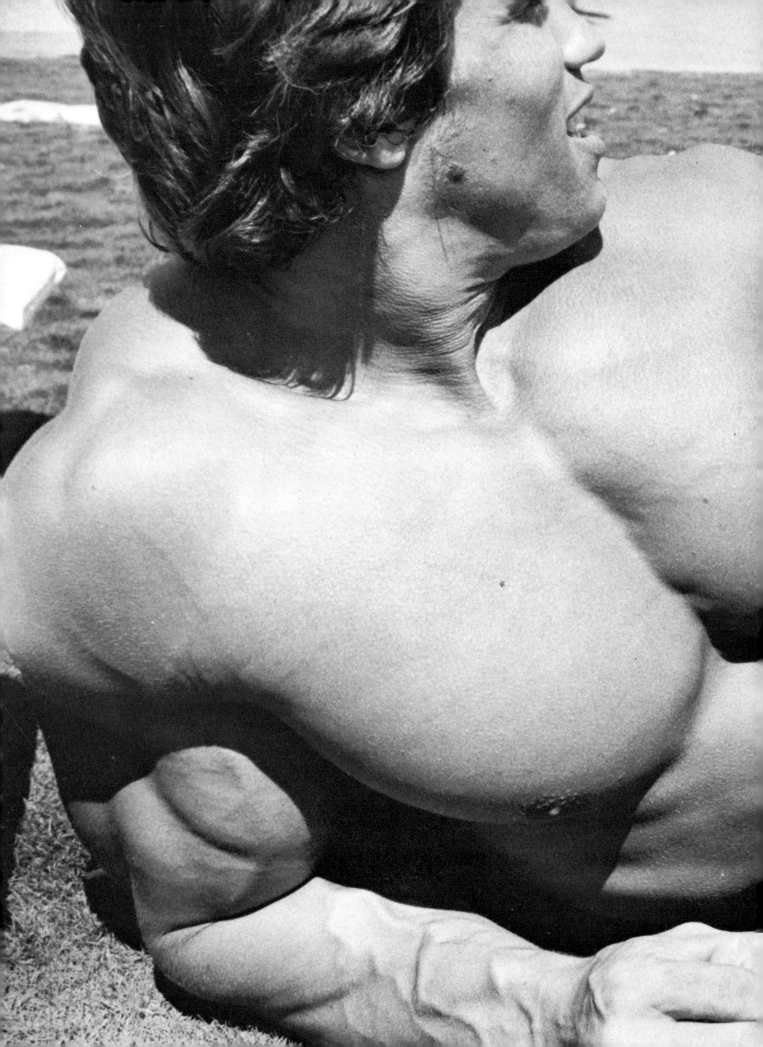

brim straw hat, a downtown hat—mimicking black jive talk with his deep, Nazi voice.

"Goawnn, Arnold," says the owner of the hat, cracking up.

Spurred, Arnold begins a series of imitations, getting each exactly, and devastating the girl on Denny Gable's back. She sits astride Gable in a bikini, rubbing coconut oil into his shoulders, playing dust to Arnold's vacuum cleaner. Evidently she walked into this cold; she is not one of the groupies who hang around here—like the carnivorous-eyed males lolling nearby with cameras around their necks—just to get a glimpse of him. Nobody told her she was going to run into one of the most magnetic men in the Western world today, and she is fairly humming. But Arnold is used to that. There's nothing new there and it doesn't affect his performance. Midway into it he decides he needs oil himself and he asks Kent Kuehn for some. Kuehn, prone on his stomach, mutters into the grass that he doesn't have any.

Arnold shakes his head solemnly. "They all haff it in the back of their minds, these guys, to knock off the King," he says.

Just then, into the thick of this, from somewhere out of the California afternoon wanders an alligator wrestler from Florida with a knife at his hip, looking, perhaps, like a real assassin. He seats himself carefully on the bodybuilders' grass, crosses his legs, and only then looks around—plaintively at first like a hit dog, his eyes whirling with dope; but then as he begins to focus on these people around him, and particularly on the unreal one with the hat, this alligator wrestler, this typical segment of the outside world, commences hysterically and uncompromisingly to *stare.*

A few years ago some inventive psychology course somewhere ran an experiment in alienation in which a student was made to wear a paper bag over his head to class every day for a semester. At first the other students were amused by the bagged one, but after a few weeks he began to get mysteriously on their nerves, and by the end of the semester most of them confessed to feeling all-out hatred or terror for the sonofabitch in the sack.

There are as few men built even remotely like Arnold as there are, say, Przhevalski horses or Texas blind salamanders. And nothing in modern American life had prepared that gentleman from Florida for what he was confronted with. He found himself, suddenly and hideously, in the middle of a lawn full of people with bags over their heads, and all he knew to do was stare. He is not alone. Outside of the Gold's Gyms and Venice Beaches, almost the entire civilized world stares at bodybuilders, with disgust, with fright, with awe. And a few—like the girl who ran into Arnold in a bar the night before—with pure-D ecstasy. She was backing out of the place banging a tambourine, in the company of four or five other stagettes out for a night on the town, when she ran smack into the entering Arnold. He caught

her. She turned to him, her head just above the level of his waist, and began to feel him experimentally, as though he were the back wall of a cave. She felt, paused, felt a little higher. "Je-sus Christ," she shrieked at her friends. "Come *feel* this. Look at this goddam body!"

Arnold might have told her, Look, I am the supreme example of an art form for which there is hardly an audience in this country. Or: What you are now feeling is a body, yes ma'am, but it is also an athletic product like Catfish Hunter's slider or Ken Rosewall's backhand, the result of years of disciplined and specialized training, that you could not possibly appreciate fully until you have seen it on a stage, doing what it does in competition.

He could have said something like that, but instead he just grabbed back. She knew how to look, this girl. And a bodybuilder's whole world breaks cleanly as a saltine into those who know how to look and those who don't.

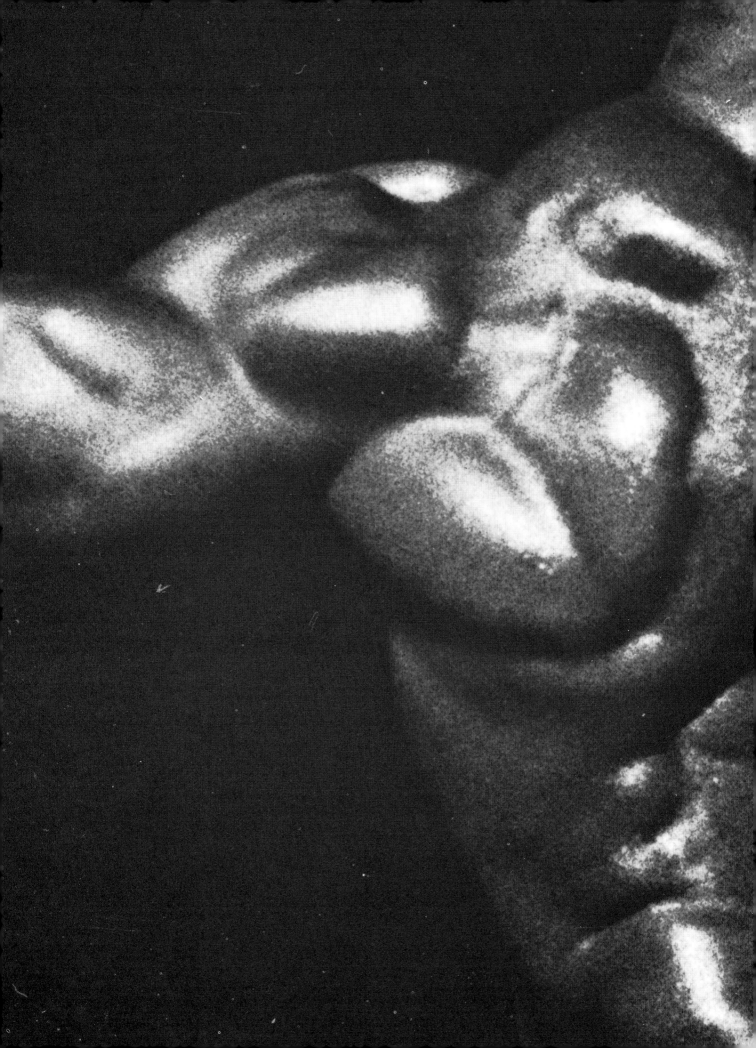

Part Two
The Competition

Art completes what nature cannot bring to a finish.
The artist gives us a knowledge of nature's
unrealized ends.

—Aristotle

Bodybuilding as such is not really a sport at all.
It's a very serious performance of art, I believe.

—Sigmund Klein

Seven

If a sport is a physical activity that human beings train for in order to compete at, then bodybuilding is certainly a sport. And yet Sig Klein is right: more importantly and interestingly, it is also an art form; and one of the things that bother the millions who don't know how to look is a confusion over how and where these two meet. Since very few of those people have ever been to a body contest, they have no way to understand how having muscles can be a competitive thing; and since they live in a time when the male body is generally not regarded very highly, and practically never in aesthetic terms, it is just as difficult to imagine how it can be an artistic thing. They are used to sports where the body is a means, not an end in itself, and it seems effete to a lot of them for a sport to require nothing more of the body than just to be presented for viewing. "What are all those muscles good for? I mean what can those guys *do* with them?" are the sort of practical questions you hear.

The fact is they can usually do a lot of things with them; that is a fact but not the point. The point is that the nature of bodybuilding competition is aesthetic rather than athletic. There are other sports where artistic judgments determine the competition—like diving, and show riding, and figure skating, and free-style skiing. And there are still others, like tournament fly casting or skeet shooting, where the skills being tested are as divorced from their practical applications as a bodybuilder's muscles are from the work they can do. Bodybuilding is a little like those sports. In its stylization of movement and concern with ritual it is also a little like bullfighting. But largely it is unlike anything else, and to be really able to enjoy it, to learn

Glenn McMahan

"I'd wear a half leotard—sometimes I'd have a red one, I had different colors—and Roman sandals. And I did, first I'd do the muscle posing, classical posing; muscle control, uh, hand balancing and then juggling of weights —kettle weights, dumbbells and barbells. First you take 'em and spin 'em—from left to right. Then you reverse 'em. Then a double spin. Then you throw it over your shoulder and catch it in front of you. . . . They'd weigh sometimes from 25 to 35 pounds, more heavier if you do 'em right. Then you take the kettle bell, throw it behind you and catch it over there. You go between your legs and spin and catch it here. And then you learn other little tricks with it. I'd often wind up by hanging it on my little finger and I'd have a kid hold a cardboard and I'd write my name, Klein, in black letters.

"All right. That was the kettle bell. Then with the dumbbell, you'd do other things. I'd swing it up, right? And I'd let it spin and catch it on the sphere. Now there'd be one sphere there on my hand, right; the other one's way up on top. From there I'd spin it and catch it on the handle, and then I'd throw it into this hand, then into that hand. Then I'd let it drop into the crook of the arm. I'd spin it around, catch it here, and do that several times. Then I'd spin it in front of me this way. Then I'd lift it up and put it behind my head on the shoulders . . . and then tilt it off and spin it around real fast. And with a barbell . . . I'd often take the whole barbell and rest the sphere on the palm of the hand and then

how to look (if you don't just naturally know how like the stagette in the bar), it is helpful to begin with a couple of basic suppositions.

First, for anyone who would like one, here is a definition: contest bodybuilding is athletic training of the body for artistic competition. To enjoy or understand it you need to suppose, first, that the male body is a potentially beautiful thing, capable of being worked and perfected like a piece of sculpture, and, second, that the product of that work can be a serious subject for contemplation and visual enjoyment.

These may be unfashionable things to suppose, but they are not at all new. At certain periods of Western history they were taken for granted, and the two major peaks of our visual culture, the sculpture of fourth- and fifth-century-B.C. Greece, and the painting and sculpture of the Renaissance, were based on and inspired by a vision of the perfected male body as the single most articulate and satisfying form in nature. A similar vision, an imaged idea of the potential formal beauty of flesh, lies at the root of bodybuilding, both as sport and as art—from the time some skinny fourteen-year-old with Tareytons rolled into the sleeve of his T-shirt picks up his first barbell to make his arms a little bigger, until years of training later when, if he is very lucky and good and unsparing with himself, his body might come together in a certain pose and everyone watching will think he is seeing that particular configuration of the human form for the first time ever.

From the beginning a bodybuilder works with himself as a medium, in much the same way that Praxiteles or Phidias or Michelangelo worked with bronze and Carrara marble—formalizing and idealizing his material, dispensing with its imperfections and forcing an idea of it into design. In his work he is after the same basic qualities of balance and clarity that those artists were after, so it is not surprising that often the result of his work is strikingly like the sculpture and painting of classical and Renaissance artists.

The schematized architecture of abdominal, oblique, serratus and pectoral muscles developed by Polycleitus in the fifth century B.C. (which became so accepted a disposition of those muscles that it served as a model for the cuirasse, or torsopiece of armor) could have been lifted directly off Franco Columbu. In the Metropolitan Museum there is a Roman bronze of the Emperor Trebonianus Gallus whose rib cage and thighs look exactly like Mike Katz's, and a Hellenistic statue of the Drunken Herakles with a right leg like Ken Waller's. The Farnese Hercules statue in the National Museum in Naples, Michelangelo's figures of God and Adam on the ceiling of the Sistine Chapel, and his magnificent statue of Day on the tomb of Giuliano de' Medici, as well as any number of other works by Hellenic, Hel-

press it up slowly. And that was
quite a balancing stunt—to hold
that old barbell up there like
that."
——Sig Klein

Sigmund Klein
73 years old
5'4½" tall
148 lbs.

lenistic, Roman and Renaissance artists, look as though they might have been painted or sculpted using contemporary body-builders as models.

It is easy to make more out of these kinds of similarities than ought to be made. Franco Columbu has probably never heard of Polycleitus or a cuirasse, and I know for a fact that he doesn't think of himself as walking sculpture. The point is that, like the humanist artists of classical Greece and the Renaissance, he is involved in transforming the human anatomy into an instrument of expression; and that while his training is athletic (more gruelingly so than that for any other sport except maybe long-distance running), the product of it is not a speed or a skill but his own body, reorganized and rendered into something which has to be looked at and evaluated aesthetically to be appreciated, and which should be able to provide at least as much pleasure when studied that way as a piece of marble twenty-five centuries old that resembles it.

The problem for a lot of people in taking that pleasure, of course, has to do with the fact that Franco is made out of *flesh* —a stuff that pulls at our most intimate emotions and memories in a way marble can't. Those humanist artists, after all, weren't really sculpting or painting men, but Man, right?—at times in history when people believed in him—showing him muscular with dignity, achievement and the possibilities of the species. It was all sort of *symbolic,* and looking at that kind of thing is a damned sight different from looking at some raffish, beefed-up ex-bricklayer Sardinian.

"God, these guys are *gross.* I mean . . . *God,*" she said.

She was a secretary at the William Morris Agency in New York City and she was looking through a stack of Butler's photographs which she had asked to see, turning them over one by one with a single two-inch fingernail as though they might be infected.

We had been this route before and knew the lines.

"Why are they gross?"

"Do they really look like this? I mean that's just . . . that's just . . ."

"How about sculpture? How about those Greek and Roman statues at the Metropolitan with all the muscles?"

"That's different. That's aht." She finished the stack, sighed. "Aht isn't human."

Maybe not. But I can think of a number of times when it was very hard to tell the difference between them. Like one hot Sunday afternoon at the Mountain Park Amusement Center in Holyoke, Massachusetts. Outside the auditorium or pavilion as it is called, a roller coaster clattered up and down a wooden trestle. Children flew around on little whirly things that looked like boats with wings. There were clam bars, pizza stands, dart throws, cotton-candy booths and a Commando Machinegun stall. Inside, on the stage in front of twelve hundred people, Leon Brown, a black laundry worker from Staten Island, was posing for the 1972 Mr. East Coast title. He had come on stage in a high-chested glide, his mouth a little ajar, his eyes flat with concentration, and stared for a long moment into the rear of the huge auditorium as if somebody back there were trying to teach him canasta. Then he found whatever it was he was looking for and began a routine that was right on top of perfect. Somewhere toward the middle of it he slid into a back pose and jiggled it tense—trapezius, deltoid, infraspinatus, lats, all the workhorse muscles of the back, coming together suddenly like the click of a box and gleaming above his white posing trunks like oiled chocolate in perfect organized mounds. It was the kind of pose that a bodybuilder finds only once in a while—when everything is right and he reaches for it and hauls it down, and all the muscles fall into place like gears meshing. For the people in that audience it was like seeing Leon get hit by lightning.

Learning how to look at bodybuilding is probably no more than learning how to be objective and unembarrassed about the body, enough so that you could look at that back pose of Leon's without wondering about what makes him do it, or how it smells up there, or what his sex life is like—and just go along with the visual thrill of seeing something brilliant and uniquely expressive done with the human form.

As a preoccupation of men who have wanted to make themselves stronger, bodybuilding has been around since the Babylonians. But in its present sport-art, competitive form it is a relatively recent phenomenon that seems to have grown out of the nineteenth-century European strongman acts.

Nobody tells how that might have happened better than Sig Klein.

Sig Klein is seventy-three years old. He began bodybuilding in 1919, is still doing it, and is in better shape today than most men ever get into. When he retired from business two years ago to spend more time collecting beer mugs, he closed down one of the first, and oldest continually operating, bodybuilding gymnasiums in the country—a legendary place on Seventh Avenue in New York called Sigmund Klein's Physical Culture Studio.

The history of bodybuilding, like that of any sport or art, is a history of the men who have bent and shaped it, and Sig Klein is one of them—one of the classiest. Two years ago in New York, just after he retired, he told me how he thought modern bodybuilding began, and it turned out to be a story about another one—a strongman who became the world's first physique artist:

"People say, 'Well, when did systematic bodybuilding start?' Well, the ancient Greeks had it. The ancient

Chinese had it. But how it came to the so-called civilized world—if you want to call it that, which it isn't—is another story. I believe that it got its first big push in Prussia in 1811, at a time when the Prussians had been defeated by Napoleon and were not allowed to arm their men anymore for battle. There was a man then by the name of Friedrich Ludwig Jahn who was a strict nationalist, and he said he was going to train men in physical culture to be able to defend themselves. Now, there were a lot of men that may not have been strong enough to do gymnastics, so he evolved this system of bodybuilding exercises with the weights. Moderate weights. Now, some of these fellows liked the weights more than they did gymnastics—it could be the truth, it may not be. But let's suppose that a lot of these men began to like the weights better than the gymnastics, and they started little clubs. And this spread all over Germany.

"Now I've got to come back into the story of Attila. Louis Attila was born in Baden-Baden in Germany, in 1844. It's going back quite a long time. He started in the theatrical field as a dance and song man when he was a young man. And in those days they always had professional strongmen in these different vaudeville houses. And then—speculating again—here he meets a man by the name of Felice Napoli. Felice Napoli was born in Naples—that's where he took that professional name, Napoli—in 1820. And he was the finest performer there was of strongmen feats. There were other strongmen, but never with the finesse that he had. Well, Attila wanted to get into the strongman profession, so he became an assistant to Napoli, and he learned the finest art of displaying feats of strength. Then later Attila spread out for himself and he became a very famous performer all over Europe. In 1887, at Queen Victoria's jubilee, of all the strongmen in Europe that could have been selected, they selected him as the strongman to perform at Queen Victoria's jubilee. He was presented by the Prince of Wales with a stickpin the size of a silver dollar, with a crystal painting of a little Hercules statue carved out of crystal, and thirty six big diamonds around there. Later on he had an audience at Buckingham Palace. He had royal families in Denmark taking lessons from him, and he became world famous.

"Now, at this same time there was a strongman act in London by the name of Samson and Cyclops. Samson, Charles Samson, claimed that he was the strongest man in the world, and was constantly challenging everybody to come up on the stage and lift his weights. Attila was upset with this man. He knew him very well and knew that

The *Farnese Hercules* by Glycon of Athens
(The Bettmann Archive)

Doryphorus by Polycletus *(The Bettmann Archive)*

Personification of *Day* by Michelangelo
(The Bettmann Archive)

Creation of Adam by Michelangelo
(The Bettmann Archive)

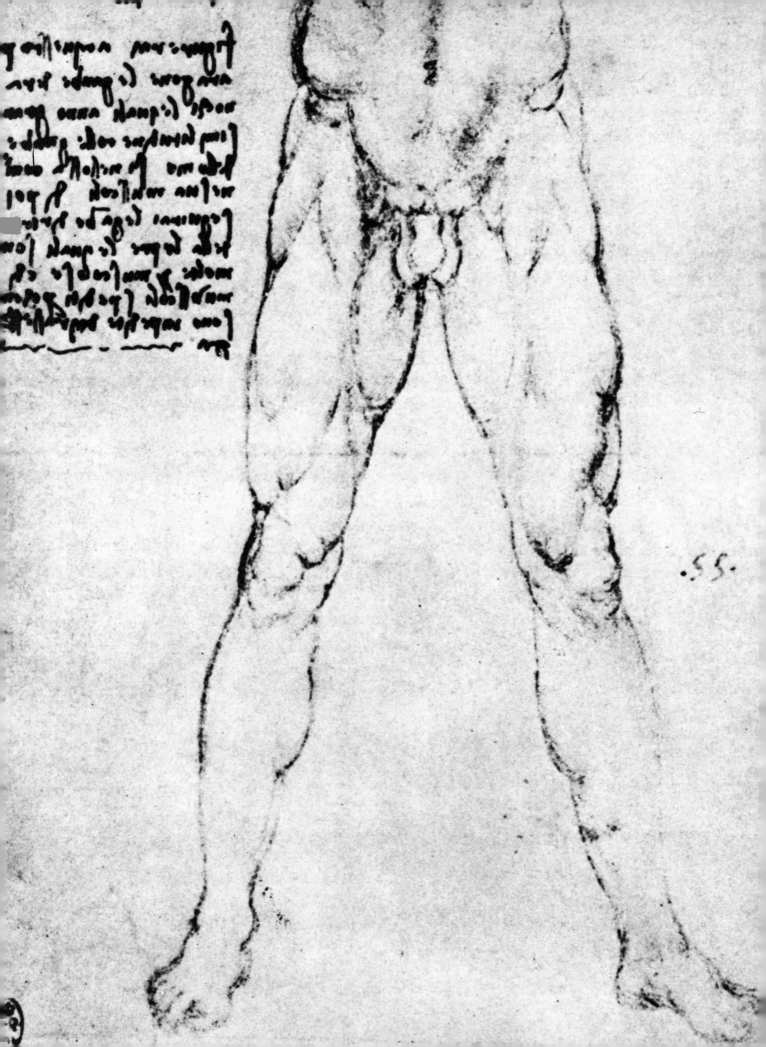

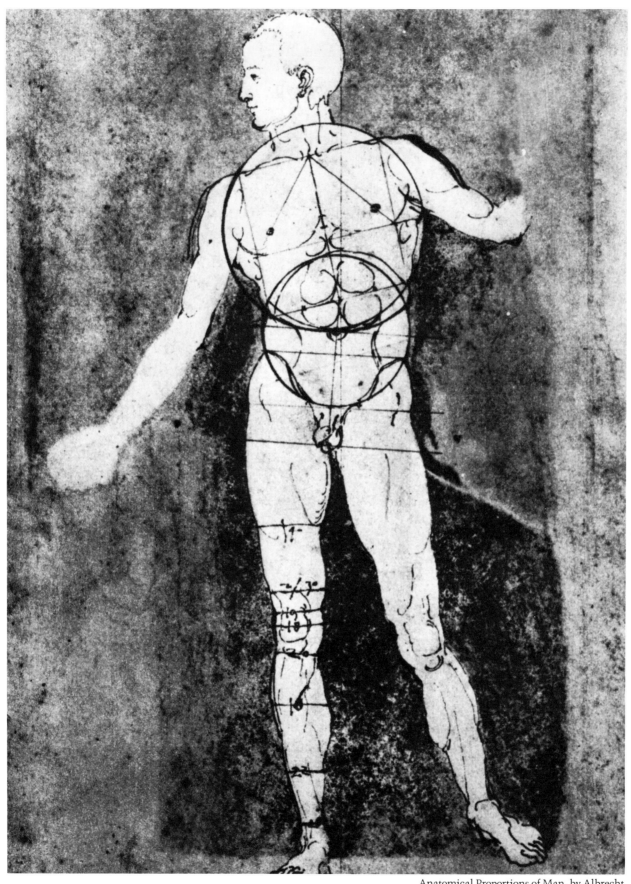

Anatomical Proportions of Man, by Albrecht
Durer *(The Bettmann Archive)*

Muscular Legs, from the notebooks of
Leonardo da Vinci *(The Bettmann Archive)*

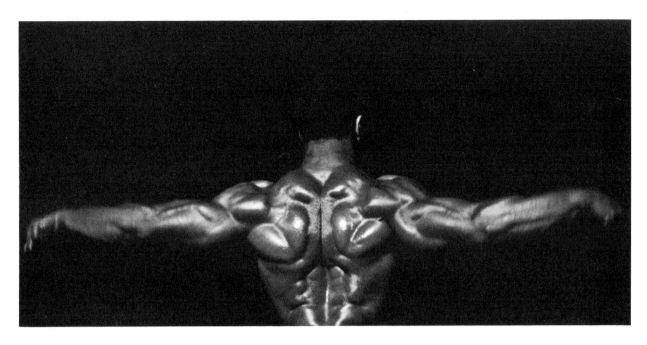

Leon Brown, back pose

*he was a braggart. Now, Attila had a school in Brussels
and he had some pupils from the Leyden University coming
there, taking lessons from him, and one of them was an
art student and he said, 'Professor, we have a model in our
class that has the finest physique that I've ever seen.'*

"Well, the professor had heard these stories before,
and he said, 'Well, if he's as great as you say he is, you
bring him to me.' And they brought a young man over to
Attila's gymnasium and his name was Frederick Muller.
And when Attila asked this young man to strip down, he
was shocked and amazed at the beauty of this young man's
form. Attila thought, I'm going to train this young man,
train him for a couple of years, and accept Samson's
challenge.

"Then finally one day Attila says, 'We're ready.' So
they get into London and Attila and this young man are
in a box when Samson makes his usual every-night challenge
and Attila jumps out on the stage and says, 'I challenge
you!'

"Samson says, 'You're going to challenge me?'

"He says, 'No. Not me. I'm challenging you for a pupil
of mine.' Attila brought the young man up on the stage.
He had him dressed in evening clothes. Beautiful blond,
curly hair.

"Samson started to laugh. He says, "This young man's
going to beat me?'

"Attila says, 'Yes. He is!' Then he had him disrobe and
the audience went wild when they saw this beautiful,
handsome, magnificent young man.

"He beat Samson, and his name was spread all over
London, of course. And then another contest was arranged,
and in England they were paying as high as fifty to a
hundred dollars for a seat in the theater to see this contest,
and the young man beat him again. This young man was
the great Sandow, and that was the beginning of his career.
Because of him gymnasiums started up, people started to
buy dumbbells all over England. And England became
the big center of the strongmen. Now the strongmen came
over from Europe, over to England, to get into the act.
Everybody wanted to make a fortune and they all came to
England, all the famous strongmen of Europe. And some
of them were much stronger than Sandow, but none of
them had the personality, the showmanship, that Attila
taught to Sandow.

"All right. Now, there used to be a firm here in New
York who were importers of big bands and big acts from
Europe. And once they saw Sandow perform they thought,
maybe we could bring him to America and make some money.

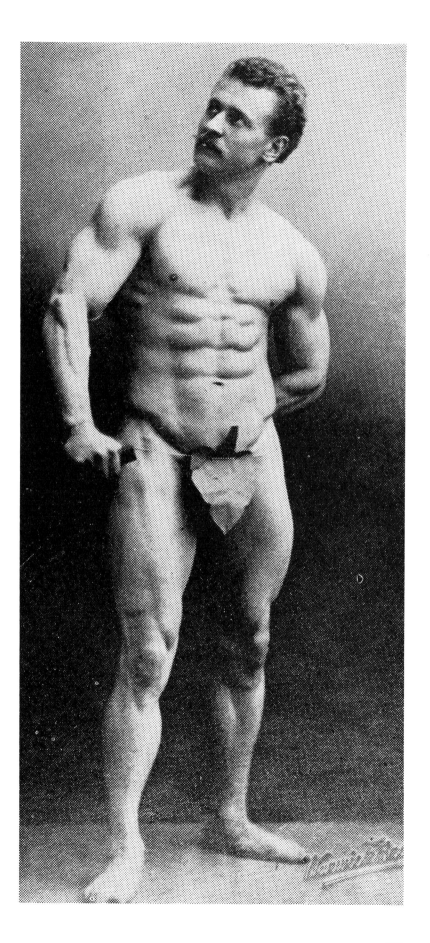

Eugene Sandow, c. 1899

Sandow lifting 19 people and a dog

Louis Cyr's one finger lift

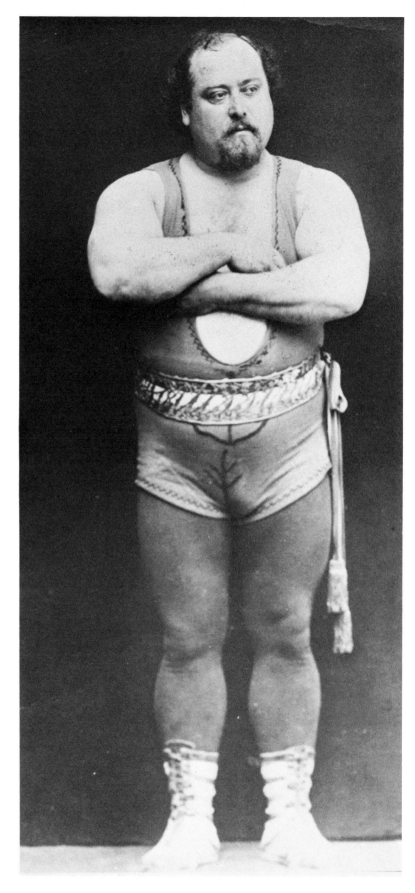

Louis Cyr, c. 1901

Eugene Caoette

They convinced Sandow to come to this country, and then when they had him here they didn't know what to do with him. But there was a young man that was getting into show business at the time by the name of Florenz Ziegfeld. The firm contacted him and they sold him Sandow's contract and thought they were glad to be rid of him. This was in 1893, at the Chicago World's Fair. But Ziegfeld had a real showmanship instinct. He took Sandow to Chicago, publicized him as the strongest man in the world, made him more famous than he'd ever been, and all over the country the dumbbells became popular.

"And that was it. That was how bodybuilding really began over here."

In his leotards, mustache and Roman sandals, Eugene Sandow happened to America at a time in Western society when appreciation of the male body was at an all-time low. Since the time of Raphael the male nude had been a distant second to the female as a serious subject of art; Victorianism had covered it from spats to chin, and the Industrial Revolution had devalued it, making

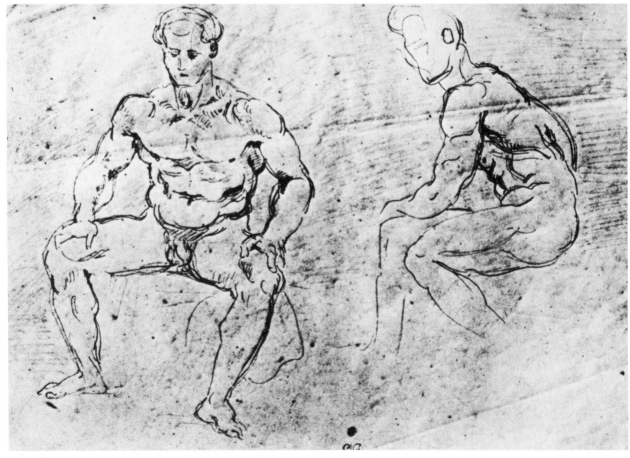

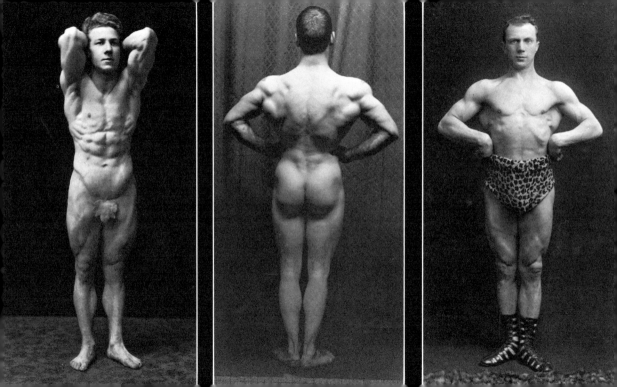

Ben Weider "discovering" Reg Park, 1947

Early representation of Joe Weider

By permission of Charles Atlas, Ltd.,
New York, New York

physical strength largely unimportant for the first time in history.

But once here, the redoubtable Sandow, just as he had done in Europe, reminded an entire male generation of what their bodies could look like and do. His physique and strength demonstrations were so popular that at one point he was earning from fifteen hundred to two thousand dollars a week from them, and, as a result of the excitement he created, bodybuilding began to enjoy the closest thing it has ever had to a heyday.

On hand at the time to help was an ex-wrestler and kinesitherapist named Bernarr "Body Love" Macfadden—the first man to stage an actual physique competition and the first in a line of publisher-promoter-businessman types who have controlled them ever since. In 1898, riding the Sandow boom and the slogan "Weakness is a crime. Don't be a criminal," Macfadden began a magazine called *Physical Culture.* And in 1903, as a promo-

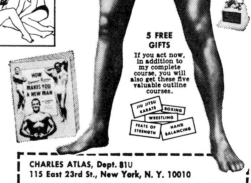

Mr. Canada Contest, 1946

"In the Guise of a Tribesman," Montosh Roy, Mr. Universe, 1951

"Dark Archer," Montosh Roy

tional device for that magazine, he put on the first physique contest ever at the old Madison Square Garden. Even at the beginning, apparently, it was hard to resist hoking up a bodybuilding competition: at the end of his show Macfadden was arrested for having "a number of toothsome women walking around the stage in their underwear."

At that first contest a physical director named Al Treloar won a thousand dollars and the title of "the Most Perfectly Developed Man in America." Nineteen years later in the same Garden, the same title was won by a twenty-nine-year-old Calabrian named Angelo Siciliano who called himself Charles Atlas, and bodybuilding took another giant step forward, smack into the tarbaby of big business.

Atlas' course in "Dynamic Tension"—the training theory he devised to get back at that immortal bully who kicked sand in his face one day at Coney Island—has sold seventy thousand copies in seven languages annually since then; and four generations of comic books have carried his ad, showing a muscular man with a big smile who seems gently amused at the world's flabbiness and asks for only fifteen minutes a day to turn it into muscle. If, as a lot of bodybuilders feel, Atlas and his ad have not had an altogether good effect on bodybuilding, they did at least and for certain introduce it to a broader public than it had had before. And, more centrally to the recent history of the sport, they served as the first irrefutable example that there was money to be made in selling muscles.

For many years Macfadden's annual competition was the only one around, but in the 1930's, with Atlas smiling and selling strongly in the pulps, contests and titles began to sprout all over America. Then in 1939, the American Athletic Union with its usual fondness for order decided to step in and regulate everything by sponsoring state and sectional competitions and a single, ultimately national one. This was the Mr. America contest, won that first year by a man named Roland Essmaker, and it marked the beginning of bodybuilding's ambiguous modern era.

During the forties and fifties—with various kinds of sanctioned and unsanctioned competitions going on all over the country, with different organizations, magazines and barbell companies being created, and with the internecine struggles that all of this new activity produced—the heretofore thin, pure history of bodybuilding becomes Byzantine with complexities that are as boring to write about as they are to hear. The highlights are enough.

Of the competitors there was John Grimek, Mr. America of 1940 and '41, a dignified man, a superb poser, and one of the three or four greatest bodybuilders of all times. And his friend and student, Steve Stanko, who was Mr. America in 1944, and who won the first Mr. Universe title in Philadelphia in 1947. In the late forties and fifties there was Steve Reeves, another Mr. America, who quit bodybuilding after he won the National Amateur British Bodybuilding Association's Mr. Universe title in London to go make Italian Hercules films and become, next to Charles Atlas, the most widely known of all bodybuilders. There were also Reg Park, and Clancey Ross, and Bill Pearl, each of whom was, at his own time, the best there was; and others like George Eifferman, Zabo Koszewski, and Armand Tanny of the old Muscle Beach group, who were good too.

Of the publisher-businessmen who succeeded Bernarr Macfadden as contest sponsors and general promoters of the sport, there were, and still are, three primary ones: Bob Hoffman, a weight-lifting coach and AAU official who publishes two muscle magazines and owns York Barbell Company and a subsidiary that sells health foods and supplements; Joe Weider, a Canadian who lives in California, and whose Weider Enterprises also controls two magazines and a barbell and food-products company; and a former CBS Sealtest Strongman named Dan Lurie, who does roughly the same things in a smaller way and heads a professional bodybuilding organization called the World Body Building Guild.

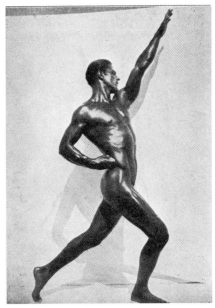

Tony Sansone, c. 1940

Atlas himself might be amazed at the size of the business these guys do. The domestic and foreign circulation of the Weider magazines, for instance, is over a million; and the yearly advertising budget for only one of Weider's dozens of products, a cable body-shaper, is nearly three million dollars. All of them have become wealthy because of bodybuilding. All of them sell their companies' products through their respective magazines, and all of them use bodybuilders or ex-bodybuilders to advertise those products. Given all of that in common, you would think they'd have a lot to say to each other. But the fact is—and it is a damaging fact to bodybuilding—they don't, and whatever they have to say about each other generally falls into the category of slander.

Of the organizations that followed the AAU into bodybuilding, the most important is the International Federation of Bodybuilders, based in Montreal and run by Joe Weider's brother Ben, who is probably the most selfless of the men now involved in promoting the sport and unquestionably the one who has done the most to advance it. The IFBB is a well-run international organization and the eleventh largest sports federation in the world, with eighty-three member nations, all of which stage physique contests. In addition to it and the AAU in America there is Lurie's WBBG, and in England there is the twenty-five-year-old National Amateur British Bodybuilding Association, or NABBA, a private operation.

John Grimek, 1941

Again, it would seem logical for these organizations to coop-

Steve Reeves, 1947

erate for the good of the sport. They don't. Each prefers to pretend that the others don't exist. And because of the traditional absence of cooperation and goodwill between them, bodybuilding in this country has stood virtually still in almost every important way since 1950. There are more contests around, a little more cab fare, and arms now are over twenty inches. But the big things, the *big* things—the shoddy contests and the magazines that reinforce the general public's image of physique competitions as deviant exhibitions in seedy basements full of wine-drunk voyeurs, the insularity that allows all the various myths about bodybuilders to continue, the petty organizational jealousies and resentments that keep them from entering whatever competitions they want to enter, and the nasty fact that despite all the cash around it is still impossible for any but the one or two best builders in the world to make anything like a living at the sport—have stayed the same. And they wouldn't have if some of those organizers and promoters had been doing a little less scratching and hauling for themselves and a little more for the sport.

One thing that has been accomplished since the forties is the creation of a welter of new contests. But because many of these are mutually exclusive, because a number of the titles are identically named, and because the organizations that sponsor them refuse to work together for an overall system of competition, the results have not been of any great benefit to bodybuilders. To anyone else the results can seem downright ludicrous.

Here is a list of the major amateur and professional bodybuilding titles given every year and the organizations that award them. There are literally thousands of lesser titles conferred annually in America—state, city and regional titles, titles like Mr. Boiled-Peanut Festival, or Mr. Miracle Mile. These are the big ones.

Dave Draper, Mr. Universe, 1966

Jean-Louis Auger,
Modern Canadian strongman

 AAU: Mr. America, Mr. World, Mr. U.S.A.
 IFBB: Mr. America, Mr. World, Mr. Universe, Mr. Olympia
   (professional).
 WBBG: Mr. America (professional), Mr. World (professional),
   Mr. Galaxy (professional).
NABBA: Mr. Universe, Mr. Universe (professional).

In 1973, Jimmy Morris of the AAU, Lou Ferrigno of the IFBB, and Chris Dickerson of the WBBG, were *all* Mr. Americas, Dickerson for the second time, since he had already won the AAU version of that title. Roy Duval, Ken Waller and Boyer Coe were all Mr. Worlds, Coe for the second year in a row and after having also been an AAU Mr. America, and Waller after having been the IFBB Mr. America. Coe, Dickerson and Ferrigno (who had been

Courtesy of *Muscle Builder Magazine*

Courtesy of
Strength and Health Magazine

Courtesy of *Iron Man Magazine*

an IFBB *and* a WBBG Mr. America but never an AAU, because they won't let you in if you've been in the other two, any more than the IFBB will if you've been in a WBBG contest before theirs, or in an NABBA either for that matter) were the three Mr. Universes.

All of this, of course, makes perfect sense to a bodybuilder. He knows that some of these titles mean more than others, and which ones have what significance—knows, for instance, that of the amateur titles the IFBB Mr. Universe and the older NABBA one are now the most prestigious, having replaced the AAU Mr. America; and that the Olympia is the top contest of all, that the chances are excellent that whoever holds that title in a given year is the best bodybuilder alive, the true Mr. World, Galaxy and Universe. But to ordinary people (among them all the fans that bodybuilding presently doesn't have), it appears laughable and meaningless to have so many puffy, interchangeable-sounding designations floating around, and to have so little, well, hierarchy or something to the whole thing.

And so it is. But a meaningful and sensible titular structure, like a number of other things bodybuilding needs, could result only from all those acronymic groups living together, and for the present they are not willing to do that. Besides, none of them has ever worried too much about what the ordinary people think anyway.

Few things are more fascinating or moving to human beings than bodies. We all have one and covet others; we look to them for pleasure and gratification, for sensory information, for protection and flight and communication. We stare at them, fondle them, make love to and with them, develop fetishes about them, indulge them, ponder them. And at some point we all, every mother's son or daughter of us, *care about how ours looks.* Furthermore, most of us care in a cheerfully Platonic way—granting, every time we notice that we are too fat or have good calves, the existence somewhere of an ideal waistline, an ideal calf.

Given the fascination and the inclination to idealize, it should be perfectly natural for people to find interest in bodies that have been developed and worked as far as the medium of flesh will allow—that are not only bodies but symbols, every bit as universal and articulate as carved marble or bronze, of our physical potential and limitation. It should be, and in Asia, the Middle East and parts of Europe, places where bodybuilding is vastly more popular than it is here, it seems to be very natural indeed. Perhaps it would be in America too, where almost all the best bodybuilders are, if it were not for the fact that bodybuilding over here has seemed determined to keep itself a secret. Ever since Sandow hung up his leotards, the internals of the sport seem almost to have conspired to keep this one, simple truth from

THE ADVANCED MUSCLE AND POWER BUILDING MAGAZINE   CHAMPIONS BELIEVE IN

MUSCLE

25p

MAY/$1.00
K 48632

BUILDER/
POWER

The Weird, Uncanny way
Arnold Schwarzenegger
**DEVELOPED HIS
MIND-BLOWING CALVES!**
Completely Illustrated Course
by Joe Weider, his Instructor

Gene Mozēe Asks: **IS CHEMICAL
BODYBUILDING THE ANSWER?** He
Questions the Top Stars! It's All Here...

6 Weeks of Weider Techniques Caused
KENT KUEHN's TRANSFORMATION
From a Fairly Good Bodybuilder Into a
"Mr. U.S.A." Winner! He Tells You How
He Did It...

Why The **AMERICAN BODYBUILDING
MOVEMENT** Is Still Screwed-Up! Facts
Letters—Exposé—Everything You Should
Know!

DON'T TOUCH THE BIG "O" It's the Only
Contest that Settles ALL Arguments
About WHO Really is the "Greatest of
All," says Rick Wayne, Mr. World
and Mr. Europe Winner!

The World's **WEIGHTLIFTING
CHAMPIONSHIP REPORT** by Oscar
State, General Secretary
International W-L Fed. (While
American Bodybuilders take First 3
Places in International Competition,
thanks to the Weider System,
Weightlifters take 13th at World's
Championships; The Worst
Showing, thanks to Hoffman
and the AAU Setup!)

**The Greatest MONSTER
MUSCLESHOW EVER!**
Like a Pack of Lusting
Sharks Sensing Blood,
3,000 Muscle Fans Witness
Arnold Win "Mr. Olympia"
the 4th Time!... Ferrigno
Win "Mr. America!"...
Waller Win "Mr. World!"
It's All Here—Photos
—Story—the Exciting Drama!

**LOU FERRIGNO—
"MR. UNIVERSE" WINNER!**
You've Read Enough Bunk
About Him—but In This
Exclusive Interview,
Louie Tells It as It
Is to Joe Weider!

LOU FERRIGNO
IFBB Mr. America and Mr. Universe

getting out: for whatever reasons, a physique competition is *fun* to look at. And at its best—when the show is right, when a posing routine is being laid down exactly right by a first-class body-builder who has everything together—it can be something else as well. Then you don't have to be reminded of Phidias or any of those people to swear you are watching something very much like art.

Joe Weider at work

Ben Weider: President, IFBB

Franco Columbu

Eight
Mr. Olympia No. 3

There is no question on which side are the two thousand people swelling the Brooklyn Academy of Music for the 1973 IFBB Mr. America, Mr. World and Mr. Olympia contests. From the Miss Americana contestants backstage, fighting over pens with which to give away their addresses, to the iridescent fags glimmering quietly in the great dim lobby, this one four-thousandth of New York knows exactly how to look. Expert, persnickety, rabid— these people are fans.

They have been here now for three hours, watching speeches, presentations, balancing acts, and over fifty amateur bodybuilders in the first two contests. They have just witnessed the strange and determined expiration on stage of Serge Nubret. They are ready to be plied.

The cheering starts before Martin Stader can finish the introduction, and it continues through the full two minutes that Franco Columbu allows the empty stage and the audience to wait for him. Franco wants them ductile when he comes out. He has listened to Nubret's applause, knows he died, and is not surprised. He and Arnold Schwarzenegger put it to the Lion a little bit backstage, not pumping up while he did, walking around in shorts to show Nubret what Gold's Gym legs are like. Little things, to help him psych himself. Franco didn't know it then, but it wasn't really necessary. Nubret had already had all the psyching he needed.

An hour before the prejudging that afternoon there was already a crowd clustered around the back door of the Academy. It was a colorful mixture of Lafayette Square dudes, photographers, fid-

"When I'm on the stage I control everybody down there in the audience. I'm very secure about myself, and I think I am much higher than anybody there because I'm on the stage doing the work. And they are watching me. They paid to see me. And I'm very confident. Very, very confident. And I, I show much possibility. I'm not afraid of anything. I am very secure."
—Franco Columbu

Serge Nubret arriving,
Brooklyn Academy of Music

gety tight-skirted groupies, and an assortment of bodybuilders who lounged against the building and on the customized cars, arms folded on their chests, eying each other lazily. And suddenly there was Serge Nubret, big as a house, getting out of a limousine with his glamorous wife, Jacqueline, and his manager, a chubby Spanish cosmetics executive named Paco. Now, you talk about *class*—a rich foreign manager with a briefcase, a limo, and a dynamite wife in a sherbet-green blouse! The crowd stiffened appreciatively, milled, angling for looks. Nubret sidled into it, followed by his wife and manager. He gave out a couple of obligatory handshakes and stood for a moment on the sidewalk talking remotely, his hands crossed at his crotch, his dark face somber, like Senator Hugh Scott holding a news conference— looking, well, a little *embarrassed* by all this and more than a little put out. Then with Jacqueline on his arm he made his way abruptly into the Academy, leaving a definite and lingering impression of downright uppityness out on the street.

But it wasn't arrogance Nubret was showing the people out there. To understand what it was, as well as what happened to his posing routine later that evening, you would have had to see him the afternoon before in Tom Miniechiello's gym, where he ran into a photographer with pictures of the competition. Nubret had come in friendly and relaxed for a protein drink or two and some conversation with the boys in the gym. Jaqueline perched herself eloquently on a couch. Paco began showing pictures of naked women. Dressed in black, Serge had stood in the middle of the lobby and thumbed through some recent photographs of Franco and Arnold—his right hand shaking noticeably, everything going bleak on him all at once.

When Franco does come out it is right now. In a hop he is on the posing dais, thick as a howitzer shell, hitting shot after shot. *Bap, bap, bap.* Franco's routine is like a speedbag workout— quick and ferocious, with a loud, fast rhythm. He gets off twice as many poses as Nubret, without hurry and without missing a move, coming off the line of one with sharp, precise motions that stab into the next: squat, thick, dramatic poses that don't try for length or flow but make the most of his overall development and the magnificent depth and clarity of his muscles. A chant begins in the audience and grows: "Franco, Franco, Franco. . ."

Bap, bap, bap, bap, bap goes the best short man in the business. And when he leaves he is close to tears.

"I was thinking when I got out there on the stage to pull the people into me and make them happy. I went out very slow and I was very, very happy with the applause. When I was going back to the dressing room, I felt inside very close to the audience. I almost cried."

"I wasn't thinking about anything or anybody in particular.
I was thinking about all of them.
What I was really thinking in the
moments when I was doing one
pose and they applause so much,
and my mind was really with the
next pose, thinking gonna be
more, gonna hit even harder and
the next one more hard, till it
was so convincing that they
would scream more and more and
more till they couldn't take it
anymore."
——Franco Columbu

Nine

Joe Disco took me to my first physique contest. It was held at the big, gaunt downtown YMCA in Birmingham. It was an AAU contest, maybe a Mr. Alabama, and there had been a powerlifting competition before it. I remember that the room was badly lighted and smelled of liniment and sweat. It had been kept cool for the lifters, and there was a lot of white dust on the floor from the chalk they use on their hands.

Disco said to pick out a particular good guy and watch what he did, not to try to flock-watch the whole bunch, because then I'd miss the point of what was going on. But I wasn't able to do that, and the main thing I remember is being visually confused by the amount of staring flesh out there on that white floor, and though I had seen plenty of guys pose before in front of the mirrors at Magic City, a little embarrassed by it too—by the way some of their feet were white with chalk, and how bare the room was, and how a few of them had goose bumps from the cold. Afterward I wasn't sure what to say to Disco, or even how to feel. I've been with a good many people at their first body contests since then, and very few of them can put a finger on what they feel after seeing real posing for the first time. One who could is a lady in New York named Virginia, and I'll tell about her a little later.

A lot of contests are held in YMCA's, though they are hardly ever good places to hold them. Most AAU physique competitions, including the Mr. America, are still pinned to the tails of powerlifting meets and they, particularly, tend to be held in Y's, boys' clubs, Electricians' Halls and high-school gyms—vacant, stage-

"I wouldn't want a woman that would have married me because of my physique, or was a sex maniac who just was a body freak, a body queen, who was just interested in rubbing suntan lotion on me and getting all hot and bothered every time she looked at me. You know, my wife is interested in personality, is interested in the real humanness of a person. We don't sit there with her admiring my physique, you know, and drooling and waiting to get to bed with me."
——Mike Katz

Front row, Mountain Park Pavillion, Holyoke, Mass.

143

Ray Delaney

Mr. & Mrs. Bob Klez

less places with bad lighting that are much more suitable to lifting than to bodybuilding.

Contests held outdoors, like the WBBG Mr. Fire Island (at which the competition is always less interesting to watch than the crowd it draws), can be fun to go to, but the flat light outside is no good for posing. In its wisdom, the WBBG has put on other shows in places like the Heisman Trophy Room in New York and the Fontainebleau Hotel in Miami Beach, and at those places it is more than just the light that is wrong.

All you really need to put on a physique contest are a deep proscenium stage, good lights and someone who knows how to work them. But all the best places have something else too. It is a quality, similar to the one that distinguishes the best bodybuilding gyms, that makes you feel while you are in one of them that physique competition is the best and most appropriate thing that could possibly happen there. The Academy of Music in Brooklyn is one place like that. Another one is the Pavillion at Mountain Park Amusement Center.

It would be hard to find a better or more symbolic place to see your first bodybuilding show than Mountain Park—which is a loud, raunchy, vibrating little island of gaudery surrounded by the clipped lawns of suburban Holyoke. It would be a Sunday in the summer or fall when you'd be there, and you might be there for the Junior Mr. America, or the Mr. East Coast—either one would be fine, because Ed Jubinville runs them both. Outside the Pavillion the roller coaster would be banging up and down its huge wooden trestle, kids would be yelling and there would be a lot of very colorful-looking people doing what they call "struttin' the booths." They dress up for Mountain Park on a Sunday.

By one-thirty the Pavillion would already be more than half filled. That would be a good time to go to the clam bar at the rear of the beamed, barnlike auditorium, get a beer in a Dixie Cup, find a seat up near the front and watch the people coming in. It's a flashy, noisy, animated crowd at the Pavillion, and most of them, even the women, you'd notice, are *big*—maybe in the same vicarious way that a lot of hockey fans are mean. By two there would be twelve hundred of them, packed shoulder to beefy shoulder in the connected wooden chairs, yelling to each other, sweating, chewing gum and watching the bodybuilders lounge in up near the judges' table (some of them carrying little bags with trunks and oil and a towel in them, and almost all of them *dressed,* Jack—a few, like Tony Roma or Tony Carroll, in clothes they design themselves); watching as they move on up to the stage and shake hands with Ed, and as they sign in and are measured for their height class; studying every move the builders make even though they might be talking to you at the same time, because they are fans and that's what they

Tall Class, Mountain Park

Ray Delaney in a single biceps

Franklin Green

are here for, to watch, and also because to them, the small-time builders and hardhats and housewives and factory workers that are bodybuilding fans here and everywhere, these builders are magical—aristocratic and significant as the Dolphins in their locker room—and because watching them, just watching them move around up there, is . . . ex*ci*ting, is what it is.

"That's Gordon Babb," one of them might tell you. "Best Back, Mr. A. And there's Franklin Green over there, the one with all the rings. Franklin's outtasight. Hey, Franklin, *baby*. You gotta see this guy to believe him—the *abs*, the *serratus* . . ."

He would probably point out Ray Delaney to you, and Bob Klez, and Martin Joyce, and tell you about Joyce's 720-pound deadlift. And for sure he would point out Leon Brown, who is often a winner at Mountain Park and always a favorite. Last summer at the Pavillion just before a contest that the crowd had Leon picked to win, the word got around that big Lou Ferrigno was there and going to enter. Lou was bulking up then for the Mr. America in the fall, and he was carrying around 280 pounds. The crowd watched noncommittally as he hulked up to the sign-in table to give his name, and then as he walked over to the leopard-skin posing dais and began stomping on it to test it for his weight. "No class," said a guy sitting next to me, watching Louie stomp. "The kid's just got no class." Later on, when another word came around that Lou had changed his mind about entering because Jubinville wouldn't pay him anything and because Leon looked too cut up, the guy turned to me again and grinned, his day made. "You see what I mean?" he said. "Class tells."

Over to the left of where you would be sitting is "the pit," the place the competitors go after they are measured, to change into their posing trunks, to oil themselves and to pump up. One nice thing about the Pavillion is that the pit is right out there with the audience and not backstage as it usually is. Here it is just a rectangular area made along one wall of the auditorium by hanging a canvas screen. The screen doesn't go all the way to the floor or the ceiling, so you can watch the bodybuilders' feet at the bottom, and dumbbells rising and falling at the top, and hear them shuffling and muttering behind it like cattle in a boxcar.

Jubinville likes to start his shows with a few preliminaries, saving the bodybuilding till last, not tacking it on like an afterthought the way they do in the AAU—just holding it back and setting you up. There might be a wrist-wrestling contest, or a benchpress-deadlift competition. And Ed would probably do his muscle-control act. Whatever it was, it would be well-managed and entertaining. And as you sat there with your beer watching it and listening to the crowd, with the bodybuilders off in the pit to your left getting ready, you still wouldn't know what to

Pose-Off

expect of a physique contest, but you would know without doubt that you were in the right place to see one, whatever it was.

Arnold arriving,
Brooklyn Academy of Music

George Butler and Virginia and I got to the Brooklyn Academy of Music about an hour before the prejudging was due to start There was already a good crowd out back around the stage door, talking and enjoying the hot September sun. A lot of the New York bodybuilders were there, and a few of the ones from California, and some people we hadn't seen since Baghdad: Winston Roberts was there from Canada, and Mike Katz. Everybody was having a fine time, standing around in the sun and seeing people they hadn't seen since the last big show.

I introduced Virginia to Mike. He was leaning on a car with his big arms crossed on his chest, dressed quietly as he always is, in a way that mutes his size and proportions. He shook her hand and grinned down at her in a pleased, gentle way, as though he had been hoping just that morning to meet her. A few minutes later he asked me if that was my wife.

"No. An old friend from Alabama now living in New York."

"Some old friend. She's dynamite."

"She wants to know about bodybuilding. But she can't come tonight, so she wanted to see the prejudging."

"The prejudging definitely wants to see her, too."

There was a nice breeze blowing, and the sky was very blue for New York. Leon Brown arrived. And then Kent Kuehn and Denny Gable and some of the others from Gold's. Serge Nubret pulled up in a limousine with his wife and manager, and did not dawdle on the street. After a while the man at the stage door who checks the passes said they were about to get it going upstairs, and almost everyone moved in, leaving the sun and a few girl friends and groupies and kids outside.

"Everybody here seems to know everybody else," Virginia said as I followed her in through the metal doors. "It's like a kind of party. And everybody's so . . . sweet."

She went to college at Sweet Briar, or Randolph-Macon, one of those schools in the state of Virginia that used to specialize in debutantes, which she was—and particularly in lovely ones from good Southern backgrounds, which she also was. Now, after six or seven years in New York, she was still unmarried, still had that musical variation of the Southern accent that belongs like a facial feature to a certain class of women down there and that gives each word a deep whiskey color, and still walked and tossed her head as though she were doing those things on a country-club tennis court early in the morning. Mike Katz was not the only person around who enjoyed looking at her. People had been doing that all her life, and if the looking made some of them ignore or forget how smart she was, that had never been Virginia's fault.

We took the elevator up to the auditorium level in a crowd of bodybuilders and contest officials and walked with them down the long concrete corridor, past the pit room where the Mr. America competitors were getting ready, to the stage. Tommy Miniechiello, who runs the America-World-Olympia show when it is held in New York, was trying to get the judges together at a table and adjust some big klieg lights at the same time. Behind him on the stage a lot of people were milling around—bodybuilders, and photographers, and a few of the Miss Americana contestants, already in their bikinis and stiletto pumps. Virginia and George and I went out into the big, nearly deserted auditorium and sat in the fifth row. Virginia crossed her legs and settled into the seat as naturally as if she were there to hear Richebourg Gaillard McWilliams speak on the history of Mobile.

"Now, Chawes," she said, looking through her purse for something, "I want to know about *everything* that happens."

A prejudging in bodybuilding is the contest. What is called the contest is really a show whose results have already been determined the morning or afternoon before by the prejudging. Prejudgings are held only for the big competitions, and though they lack some of the drama and the crowd reactions of the contests, they are often more interesting to watch, and they will always teach you more about bodybuilding. In that way they are rather like the school-figure part of skating competitions —the technical, straight-faced part where the nature of the competition is more apparent, where it is easiest to determine what exactly is being judged and how.

In all IFBB contests except the Olympia, which has no divisions, a prejudging begins by dividing the contestants into three height classes: the short men, who are less than five feet five; the mediums, between five five and five eight; and the tall men, who are over five eight. Depending on the contest, from three to six places are awarded within each height category, and the overall title winner is chosen from the three class winners. In most competitions there are also awards given for best individual body parts—best arms, legs, chest, back and abdominals—as well as a best-poser trophy. All of this makes for a lot of evaluating, and in a show like the America-World-Olympia, where over fifty bodybuilders have to be looked at in a space of three hours or less, the prejudging has got to be very well organized from the beginning.

The judges (there are always either five or seven) do their judging in three rounds from a table placed about twenty feet from where the builders stand. They judge the short class first, then the mediums and talls, and finally a pose-down between the three class winners for the overall title.

Round one for each height category is a nonscoring preliminary assessment round where the competitors simply parade

*"If another man can do it, so can
I. And I'm going to do it. I don't
care how much work it takes.
Work doesn't bother me. She
knows. I work hard—I go through
pain, unbelievable suffering,
and I love every minute of it.
Not because you like it—you
don't enjoy it, but somehow you
want to feel that pain in order
to know that you're having a
good workout. Believe me it's
hard work. I don't think there's
any sport in the world, anything
in the world, that takes so much
pain and so much struggle and so
much motivation. And the man
that can stand this can achieve
the top."*
—Tony Roma

"Onstage I'm always different than offstage. I can be very friendly offstage, but onstage I will pull one trick after another on my competition to wipe him out, you know—because it's my living and I have to win. Franco is my best friend, but I will do as much as I can to make him look bad and me look good."
— Arnold Schwarzenegger

"I've had phone calls, letters and personal approaches. How they got my number I'll never know. But they want you, they're going to get you. And I had phone calls and phone calls from people, and maybe I'm stupid because I would not act offended towards these people, because I felt they are human beings as well as I am, and I will just explain to them: 'Well this isn't my bag. If you're interested in developing your body I will help you, but as far as anything else goes, I'm not interested.' But maybe the word got around that I was a softie. You know, who knows? So then I got calls and calls, and the letters came. 'Steve, send me photographs of you in leather pants.' 'Steve, send me photographs of you with nothing on; I'll pay any price. I'll pay any price. I'll pay anything.' If I wasn't married and I was homosexual, I could be living for nothing. Putting my entire salary away. I could have any car I want. I could be living in . . . I've had offers to live in Maine. I've had offers to live on Fire Island. I've had offers to live in people's apartments on 86th Street down here, which is a fantastic neighborhood."
—Steve Michalik

in front of the judges, who use the first of seven worksheets to make notes about them. In round two the height class again comes out as a group and stands without flexing or posing, giving the judges front, side and back views as they are requested. The judges are free here to isolate any number of builders at a time for comparisons—asking, maybe, to see "seven and four from the side again," or "numbers one, eight and six men from the back." They are looking in this round less for muscularity than for proportion, symmetry and general appearance, and each judge scores each competitor from 1 to 20 according to what he finds. In the third and final round, the builders come out one by one and each is given ninety seconds to perform a posing routine made up of both compulsory and optional poses. He must start with the compulsory poses. There are six of these: a double-biceps from the front with the abdominals flexed, a front lat spread with flexed legs, a right side-biceps and shoulder with the side of the leg flexed, a back double-biceps, a lat spread from the rear with both calves flexed, and a left side shot with triceps, chest and the left leg flexed. They are the purest poses in bodybuilding. On no one of them is it possible to cheat, and taken as a group they represent each muscle area fairly. The optional poses are in there so that a contestant can individualize, showing the judges his posing style and concentrating on the parts of himself he thinks are the best. A man with good abs, for instance, would do most frontal shots during his optional time, laying a lot of stomach on the judges. This round is scored as the second one was, and when the totals are added and all the height-class places established, the three winners—a short, a medium and a tall—are brought out again to do identical poses side by side until an overall contest winner is decided upon.

This last part is called a pose-off. It lasts for one minute. It is the minute that bodybuilders train all year for, and if all three class winners are good it is a minute you would not forget watching.

"Why do they walk like that?" Virginia wanted to know. She was smoking a menthol cigarette. We were standing at the very back of the auditorium while she did it, looking down an aisle to the stage where the Mr. America short class was parading for the judges. There were maybe a dozen people scattered through the old, frayed Victorian hall—girl friends and wives, and three fast-talking Brooklyn fans who had managed to get passes—but the place felt comfortably vacant and intimate, and exactly right for what was going on. "They do it the same way outside."

"Because they're showing themselves off. Outside and inside, but particularly now. They're showing off the result of all that work I was telling you about, so they strut with it, put it all out front. Their arms ride out like that because of the lats. You remember what the lats are?"

"Uh huh. I *like* it, Chawes. They look like show horses. Why are they all sweaty?"

"That's oil. They put it on back in that room we went past, to highlight the muscles under the lights."

"All over?"

"Mostly all over."

"What else?"

"What else what?"

"What else do they do to themselves in there, dummy?"

"Pump up. Do exercises to get blood into the muscles, to make them bigger and bring them out."

"Is that fair?"

"Sure it's fair—that's the point. But it works better for some than for others. There's a great bodybuilder from Chicago named Sergio Oliva who used to win the Olympia every year before Arnold. They say he gets smooth the first time he pumps up, at the prejudging. At night when he pumps up again for the contest all his water is gone from sweating and he looks cut up, but by then he might have already lost. Arnold says that's the way he beat him last year in Germany."

"All his water?"

"That's sort of complicated and not very interesting. A lot of psyching goes on in there, too. All these guys know each other. They meet at the same big contests every year and it's sort of like a convention. All year they're at their own gyms, and then once or twice a year they get together. They have a lot of fun in there, but there's also a lot of staring and checking out. And psyching."

"Like what?"

"Well, like say a guy is coming in this year with bigger arms and he's proud of them. Another guy might come up to him in the pit and say something like "Hey, man, you're looking great, *great.* But, hey, you sure better work on those arms." It throws him off, and that can hurt his routine. Another thing is the best ones never take off their robes or sweat clothes until the very last. Schwarzenegger sometimes won't pump up at all. He'll just hang around and watch like he doesn't need it, and that screws everybody up."

Virginia giggled. "That's awful. How about this shaving business? Didn't you say they shave all over?"

"Yeah, they do that too. If they didn't you couldn't see the muscles clearly."

"Uh huh." She put out her cigarette with a quick little stab. "Now tell me something else. Are they, uh . . . most of them, do they like girls?"

"All the ones I know. I've heard about some who don't. And there are a few around who play gay for money. But none of the big ones."

"It just seems so—at first, I mean."

"You see your deltoids and you've got things in there, and you could stick who knows what in there and it would get lost. That's muscularity. And the thigh cuts—take a look at Leon [Brown]; Leon could get his fingernails lost in the cuts of his legs. Now that's real muscularity . . . if you get that, there aren't going to be many people around who are going to beat you."
—Mike Katz

The Walk

"People think that who don't know about it. There are plenty of homosexuals who hang around the sport, in the gyms and at the contests. But most of them don't bother anybody, and the bodybuilders don't mind them. Then there are some others with money who get into managing."

"It would just be such a waste."

"What would?"

"If they didn't like girls. Like that one on the left." She pointed to one of the shorts who had been called out of the line with two others. The prejudging was into round two. The three stood without flexing, facing the judges' table. "He is *gorgeous*. What do you think would happen if I took him back to Alabama? I could take him out to the pool at the club and show him off."

"He might not like the club. But I know he'd like you."

Virginia tossed her head, smiled. "You're right," she said. "He might not like the club."

According to the rules, competitors may "not wear footwear, watches, bangles, pendants or earrings"—or anything else, for that matter, but a brief pair of posing trunks. So they come on stage like that, nervous at first, grabbing looks at the other men, and commence to show the judges their most fundamental selves. Very few smile naturally as they do this. It is supposed to be good to smile while you are posing, so most of them learn to do it, but the smiles always look studied, the way Richard Nixon's do during television speeches. And the judges look at them. Through two scoring rounds they study the bodies relaxed and posed, flexed and unflexed, and write down numbers between one and twenty to indicate what they think of them. That is the form of the competition. The essence of it is in what the judges look for, and how they assess it.

They look first for symmetry and proportion, an overall harmony of parts, the ideal notion of which hasn't changed much since the Greek sculptors: the body should still be seven and a half times the length of the head; the diameters of the neck, upper arms and calves should still be within an inch or two of each other. They also look initially for things like skin tone, posture and skeletal structure. They look at the overall size and shape and relationships of the various muscle groups, and then they look, very carefully and individually, at each one. Starting at the top of the body, they examine the neck and sometimes even the muscles of the face—Reeves and Sandow were both admired for their square, muscular jaws. Around the shoulder area they look for slope and width in the trapezius muscles, and for the two thick pillars that should be apparent where they insert into the back of the head; for density and striation in each of the deltoids and a clear balanced separation of its three sheaths. In the chest they notice how the pectoralis merges with the anterior deltoids, how squarely formed they are and how distinct are the

Prejudging

upper and lower sternum grooves that separate the muscle. When the arms are flexed there should be sharp divisions between the two heads of the biceps and the three of the triceps; they look for that, and for peak to the biceps and a horseshoe declivity at the back of each arm. They look for the iliac furrow and the linea alba in the stomach, and for the segmented carapace of muscle there that is shaped, when it is right, sort of like the shell of a turtle. They check out the obliques, and the serratus—the small knobs of muscle like chunks of rope that tie the rib cage to the lats. The back should be broad and thick, and should taper in a deep curve to the waist down the outer edges of the latissimus dorsi; and when it is flexed, the trapezius, deltoids, teres, infraspinatus and erector muscles should tighten and spring up cleanly under the skin. In the legs they want to see deep furrows between the quadriceps of the frontal thighs, and to be able to see the peroneus longus and sartorius swells, and a sort of cleft-diamond shape to the muscles of the calf.

They look at the forearms, the Achilles tendons, even the feet. Finally they look at how close all the muscles are to the skin, how striated they are and how much adipose tissue there is to blunt them. And when they are done, if they are patient and skillful at what they are doing, each competitor knows what he wants to know: that whatever he has made of himself and brought to the stage has been carefully, thoroughly seen.

Rapt, hardly moving, Virginia sat in the middle of the fifth row and watched everything that happened on the stage from the posing round of the Mr. America through the end of prejudging for the Mr. World. I wanted there to be some good stuff for her to see, and there was. In the America there was Leon Brown with his perfectly chiseled, wasp-waisted build, and his quiet polished routine; and Bob Birdsong, one of the men from Gold's, with a routine he didn't seem to understand, but looking very ripped and close to the skin; and mammoth Louie Ferrigno, who ultimately beat out the other two for the title by outsizing if not out-finessing them. In the World there was Ken Waller and Bill Grant in the tall class, and Ed Corney in the medium. From Waller and Kent Kuehn and Jeff Smith and Bill Howard she saw a lot of the flashy, fun-to-watch Gold's Gym posing, a style of wide-open shots and sweeping transitions and dramatic, down-on-one knee flourishes.

Sitting a couple of rows behind us were the three Brooklyn fans, one of them a lumpy teen-ager named Raol who never misses a prejudging in New York and who knows as much about posing as any judge does. During most of the World, Raol pelted the backs of our heads with his quick loud chatter—"That's a Draper pose . . . a Scott three-quarter back. . . . Now watch this. . . . Aw*right*, aw*right*, a Sergio double-bicep. . . . Now he'll bring it into a crab . . . Cinch it in, cinchthatmother*in*.

. . . The guy's calves are so bad in front he oughtta stay more to the sides, show the *sides*, turkey. . . ."

Then after the World the judges called a break. The prejudging had been going on for nearly two hours. After the break they would prejudge Serge Nubret, Franco and Arnold for the Mr. Olympia title. Then they would break again, for two or three hours this time, before the show began at eight o'clock. That night the Academy would be aisle-full of Raols—whistlers, screamers, moaners and booers, a nitroglycerin Academy crowd that can chill or frenzy on a second. Each competitor then would have a minute or two before them under the spot on the posing dais. The very best ones and the local favorites like Franklin Green would be met there and followed through their routines by an unimaginable din, an urgent, rhythmic pandemonium that would break some of them into sweaty, glazed-eyed transports on the dais and bring others close to tears. And a few, the inexplicable and ridiculous few who shouldn't be there in the first place but always are—the ones with no muscle, and the ones who can't pose, and the ones who come out with erections— would leave the dais feeling sorry they were in Brooklyn that evening.

Right now, except for some talking on the stage, the place was quiet. Virginia and I walked to the back again for her to smoke.

"Do they tell who won?"

"Not until tonight after the show. Nobody but the judges knows until then. But it looks like Ferrigno in the America and Ken Waller in the World. What did you think?"

"I'd like it better if there weren't so many of them."

"So would I."

"Like maybe five in each height thing, and just the best ones. The ones who aren't so good kind of . . . blur the good ones or something."

"I know. They ought to screen for the big contests, but they don't. It's one of the things they have to improve on. There are some others too."

"But, Jesus God, the *posing*, Chawes. That Leon guy is . . . is fantastic. And the ones from that place in California. And your friend, Corney—did you see me when he got through? I couldn't blink my eyes. It was like they were frozen open. His hands and everything, and the way he moves."

"He's just had a bad knee operation. He wasn't in the shape he usually is."

"It's like ballet, isn't it? The best ones, I mean."

"Sort of, but you haven't seen the best ones yet. Ed usually is, but he wasn't this time."

"You know what it reminded me of? Of Elizabethan music. No, really; a whole lot. I kept thinking of it while I was watching.

Leon Brown, putting it together

"There's something in any man that wants to be above the average. A bodybuilder is actually the most in perfection of the human body. You want to reach the perfection. To be that sets you apart from the average man—it sets you apart. You are looked up to and respected. I think we do it because . . . it takes a lot of courage, and we dare step out of the regular routine. Not many people dare. . . . We really go down to the limit, and that sets you apart. We go through all this struggle and all this pain, you know, and this is what makes me proud. I can do other things in life much easier."
——Tony Roma

Elliot Gilchrist, fifty-four years old

You know those songs, how they're raunchy and elegant and massive and delicate and surprising all at the same time? And . . . sweet? Stop it. That's just what Corney made me think of, and a few of the others. And also of horses—Tennessee walking horses I used to see at shows in Winchester."

"I'm glad you liked it."

"Their thighs look like horses. Do you have thighs like that?"

"No. Look, are you getting tired?"

"They even look like they eat alfalfa and clover. And the way they *move.*"

"Virginia?"

"What?"

"You'd better find something to hang on to for these last three."

"I haven't seen anything, huh?"

"You've seen something. But there's a lot you haven't seen."

Ken Waller, Mr. World, 1973

Ten
Mr. Universe No. 3

And crazy is what they went, exactly—all three thousand or so people inside and outside the Al-Nasr Cinema, as soon as the Mr. Universe winner's hand was lifted by Ben Weider. Crazier than crazy. The place simply imploded toward that single spot, the dais on which he stood, and from there it must have looked to him and the others on the stage like a stained tidal wave of open mouths and frantic extremities crashing at them. What they did about it was make tracks for the dressing room.

There was supposed to be protection there, a dozen badged and billied officials whose job it was to get the winners reasonably back to their hotels. But all the officials in Baghdad would have been as powerless as those were before the mad, rioting crush of hero-hungry Arabs that filled the halls and dressing rooms as suddenly as if they had been vacuumed there from the auditorium. Iraqi officials are used to hopelessness. They gave out a few desultory whacks to anyone within range and just let it go at that. And Mike Katz and Ed Corney, both half dressed and carrying huge brass trophies, were digested by the crowd in separate lumps and swept from the building into the street before they even knew that there was no order to this thing, no *plan*.

There was a jam outside the Cinema, and Corney and I looked around, momentarily not being moved, each clutching an end of one of the three-foot trophies Ed had won, like a log in open water, and saw over the heads of thousands of Arabs thousands more, in the streets, standing on top of cars—a Darryl F. Zanuck horde of crazed little people. It was not an altogether encouraging view, but Ed was still smiling gamely.

"Well, fellows," he said to the hubbub at large, "where are we going now? Who's got the car?"

I screamed into his ear, "Ed . . . Ed, maybe we better try to find our own transportation."

"Yeah. . . . I said *yeah*. But, uh, where do we go?"

There seemed no answer to that, but suddenly one materialized. Rubbing the trophy might have produced him, who knows? But there suddenly was old Hussarian, right at Ed's elbow, looking pleased as Punch, wise and capable. We were moving again, in a southerly flow of bodies. Flash bulbs were popping, and small disembodied hands, thick as mosquitoes, hovered and settled over Ed.

"Get us out of here," he told Hussarian. "Where is Mike?"

"He eees with Bootler. You, Et Carney and Meek Kitz, *very great champions.*"

"Fine, fine, Hussarian," said Ed, smiling at him. "Thank you very much."

"We go now," Hussarian said and began, with some incredible *suk* sense, to *run* through the crowd. Ed followed in his wash, hunkered over his trophies as if in a sleet storm, his blue-and-white Hawaiian shirt winking. I seriously followed Ed.

A block or two down the sidewalk Hussarian cut left through three layers of bodies to the door of a cab he could not possibly have known was there. It was a small cab, but when we finally got the doors closed there were two enormous trophies and *eight* people in it: from where I sat in the back seat, my lap full of the new Mr. Universe and odds and ends of other people, I counted them. But at least we were behind metal and glass, and the Amateur Bodybuilding Champion of the World was no longer in any danger of being trampled to death.

As the driver shot through waves of people on the street, beginning an insane, rocketing, horn-blowing fling to the hotel, I managed to find Ed's hand and shake it. He was being kissed all over by every Arab in the car who could reach him with a mouth, and handled by the ones who couldn't.

"You done it."

Beleaguered as he was, he looked gone off, inside himself. "Yeah. You know, it's like a dream? The whole damn thing is like a dream," he said.

A dream was just what the whole thing must have felt mighty like to Mike Katz too—a bad one; dismally like the one he'd had the night before, but thickened with all the bitching minutiae of reality: the lower dais on the winner's platform—his, and Suemitsue's, the Japanese who took third place, a good two feet below Corney's; the moist looks of all those Iraqis who had expected him to win; the sinking feeling of *déjà vu* from having blown his year two years now in a row; and, mostly, the nasty little burr of having lost to an older, smaller man. And riding in

IRAQI W.L & BODYBUILDING FEDERATION

I.F.B.B

ينظم

بطولة آسيا والعالم

لكمــال الاجســـام

١٥ ـ ٢٣ تشرين الثاني ١٩٧٢

Organizing

ASIAN AND WORLD

Bodybuilding

CHAMPIONSHIPS

15 . 23 NOV. 1972

Prejudging, Medium Class, Baghdad

"I don't want to die just another slob—with my name on a gravestone someplace. I want to die with my name somewhere at the top. Make a little dent in the sport I'm in, so that maybe forty years from now people will say, 'Hey, that guy was Mr. America.' This would give me enough happiness to die with a smile on my face."
——Mike Katz

The Crab

his own cab, less noisy and festive than Ed's, back to the Hotel Baghdad, Mike might well have been sick to death of dreams. He might have thought of his nice house on a wooded corner lot in suburban Hartford, of his antique car and his wife and son, and wished to be back there right *then*—out of this gone-sour fantasy of minarets and mobs and weird water and unintelligible adulation. He might have felt all that, but if he did he didn't show it. Nor did he show any bitterness—not then, nor at the Cinema, nor later back at the hotel. Katz has a built-in sense of fairness, maybe from all the years he has spent at competitive sports, and he knew this would probably be the last crack Ed would have at the Universe. More important, he knew too that on this particular crack Ed had just flat deserved to win it.

He himself had looked good, he was sure of that—better than he had ever looked before: massive and defined, his waist down and his calves up from a year ago. And he had posed well, drawing his shots out longer, making transitions with more grace and picking his poses better than ever. It was just that Corney had looked better, and Mike knew it. Every muscle in Ed's forty-year-old body was out along its rim, close to its ultimate potential. Ed had *finish:* every part of him looked achieved and finished as a goddam apple. And his posing—well, there just wasn't anybody over here, or practically anywhere else, for that matter, who was going to beat Ed Corney's posing today.

Mike didn't begrudge Ed the title, and he didn't blame the water. So when he got back to the hotel, and the manager and the manager's family came running out to congratulate him for winning, if Mike was wishing like hell for the reality of that wooded lot and his twenty-one-inch color TV, he didn't let them know about it. And five or ten minutes later when our absurd clown car screeched up and Ed got out, shedding Arabs, to shake his hand, there was no kink in Mike's grin and nothing phony in his voice when he congratulated him. Mike might not have felt all that good, but he knew as well as anybody that losing and winning have nothing to do with dreams.

Ed Corney, on the other hand, was very, very happy—happy the way a man is who has just relieved himself of a year's worth of work. He felt successfully delivered, evacuated, and good. He ate loosely that night—garbaging up, as bodybuilders call it (though not as loosely as some do after a contest; nothing like, say, the way Ken Waller garbaged up about a year later in New York after he won the Mr. World, when he put down, in order, steak, veal and chicken dinners with three bottles of wine, and then went to a different restaurant and ate fourteen pancakes). And after he ate, he and Mike went out to the nightclub down the road that had for entertainment an international troupe of strippers billing themselves as ballet. The contest *had* in fact been televised all over the Middle East. People in Baghdad

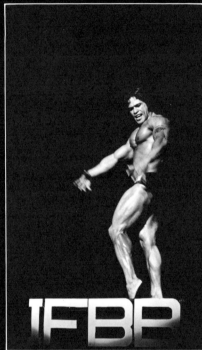

Ed Corney in competition

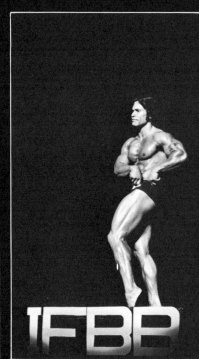

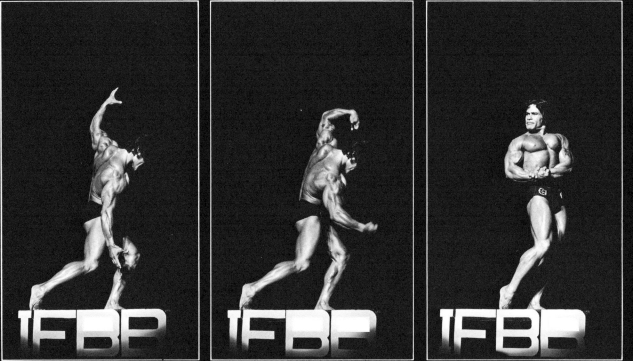

"Like any championship you go after, there's a lot of heartaches and pains that go with it, you know. There's a lot of torture; there's a lot of pain involved. Most people think all he does is train. But, you know, the pressures of life are on you . . . ups and downs. . . . You don't have a job, so you don't know where the next buck's coming from. But yet you go on training, you know? You try to find jobs. I can find just about any job I want, just like that. You're intelligent enough. And yet I don't want to work. It's not that I'm lazy; I feel that if I get a job other than bouncing, then all my attention will be toward this new thing I'm doing and I'll have to put my training aside. A lot of people don't understand that. They say, 'Why don't you go to work?' All I can say is I want to train. I'd like to have money. You know— nice things, nice things for my daughter—a nice car. But I've got a goal ahead of me and I can't reach it by making money."
—Ed Corney

watched it at home and in bars and restaurants the way we watch the seventh game of the World Series, and Ed and Mike were celebrities in the nightclub. Halfway through her act, one of the strippers, a knockout French redhead, bellied over to Ed's table, and the two of them decided in different languages that they liked each other's moves. She went back to the hotel with him that night, and the next noon when the bus left for the airport she tried to get on it with him, having decided that Fremont, California, was as good a place as any to do ballet.

Things were definitely breaking for Ed: magically almost, over here in this place where magic still felt like a hell of a lot more than just entertainment for children. Certainly the way he and Mike had been fawned over and partied, they way they'd been appreciated, by everybody from the President to the shoeshine boys outside the hotel—wasn't there some magic in *that* for a bouncer from Fremont, all of whose titles wouldn't even cash him a check back in the U.S.A., and who had been skinny more than once on luck and money? And beating out the big man, when nobody thought he could do it, and doing it this year when he had to? And even the girl in the nightclub, just when he was emptied out and loose and ready for that? And most of all, hadn't there been more than a little magic in *him* that afternoon at the Cinema? Hadn't he posed as if he owned the stage, as if no other bodybuilder had set foot on it before, moving as purely and naturally as water flowing, his fingers spreading to lead each new line, finding the lock just right on every shot? Lord, hadn't there *ever* been a little magic there.

Ed was happy all right that last night in Baghdad, and he planned to stay that way for a while. Things were breaking good. And just as Mike Katz knew about winning and losing, Ed Corney knew most of what there was to know about how fast they can break the other way.

Ten months after the contest in Baghdad, George and I were out in California, and one night we went up to see Corney at the nightclub where he works. He was standing outside the door, dressed in a pair of two-tone shoes, red knit pants, a tie and a red-and-white halter sweater. He looked very spiffy and polite and correct standing there, as though he had just taken a new girl to dinner and was waiting outside for her to come out of the ladies' room. He was holding a weighted police flashlight that he used for checking i.d.'s and also for decking people whenever he had to do that. Mostly his job there, he said, was to turn away people under twenty-one and anyone in Levi's, and anyone who looked as if he might cause trouble in the club. He thought of himself as a sort of public-relations man, he said, and he always tried to avoid putting the thumb on people. But occasionally he had to, like that past Thursday when he had told a mean-

Mr. Universe, 1972

Mike Katz back at home

"I won't do anything else until I win Mr. Universe. If I have to train ten years, I'm going to win it. I don't know why I say that because the education is just as important, but I could not be happy right now going out as a loser. I placed third in Mr. Universe last year. If I went out as a loser it would make the ten years I've spent in bodybuilding a complete waste."
——Mike Katz

drunk Persian that he couldn't come in and the Persian hit him in the mouth. They had had to carry the guy away in an ambulance, and Ed felt bad about that, but it was part of the job, when push came to shove, to hit the other guy harder than he hit you.

Ed was very cheerful and glad to see us out there in front of the club, and after a while he took us inside and introduced us to some of his friends. The club was a candlelit, semi-badass place with Formica tables and a loud rock group. Most of the people in it knew Ed, and all of them were very polite around him. He bought us a drink and himself a Coke, and we stood up in front near the door and talked. He had gotten married, he said, after he got back from Iraq. His wife had gotten pregnant right away, but she had miscarried and they had split up after that. And he had just gotten out of the hospital two weeks ago. He had had a big operation on his knee, and the thing had cut him to 150 pounds, but he was back up to 170 now and training hard. He was coming to New York in two weeks for the Mr. World contest, he said, and he figured he'd be in top shape by then.

But mostly we talked about Baghdad, reminding each other of how much fun it had been and of all the crazy things that had happened. George had brought some pictures along, and Ed looked through them, looking at each one for a long time. His favorite was a picture taken at the Hotel Baghdad right after everybody had come back there from the contest. The hotel manager asked George to take it and it shows the manager and all his family standing with Ed and Mike in the corridor outside their room. Everybody is smiling. Everybody looks happy, but Ed looks the happiest of all.

We stayed at the club for a couple of hours, talking to Corney about Baghdad and watching him do his work. Then around two we had to leave to get a borrowed car back to San Francisco. We told Ed goodbye and said we'd see him in New York. When we drove out of the dark parking lot we could see Ed Corney Mr. Universe, back outside again, standing politely and alone in front of the door to the club, waiting for i.d.'s to check.

Ed Corney outside Mr. Magooz, San Jose, Calif.

196

Eleven

Posing is the heart of the thing. Depending on how it is done, you can see in it either everything that is moving and beautiful and dignified about the display of a developed male body or everything that is ridiculous and embarrassing about it.

On its lowest level, posing is simply a technical matter of presenting the muscles, of emphasizing strong points and obscuring weak ones; and just beyond that it is an athletic skill like diving or hitting a baseball that requires timing and coordination. The great majority of bodybuilders never get beyond the point of athletic competence in their posing. Many do not even get there, and they, no matter how well developed, are always embarrassing to watch. The ones who are only competent can be interesting for one reason or another to see work, but one time is usually enough and you are hardly ever moved by them. But on its highest, most expressive level, as it is done by only a handful of people, physique posing is a kinetic form of art— requiring talent, imaginative and personal, turning on intuition —and no matter how many times you watch it performed there is always something new you can learn and feel from it.

Good posing, even great posing, is only so much movement, however interesting, unless it is displaying a first-rate physique. The physique gives the posing meaning, the posing gives expression to the physique, and the two have got to be equally finished and appropriate to each other for a routine to really grab and shake you the way the best ones can. When they are, there is nothing even remotely embarrassing or ridiculous in what you see.

What you see would look something like this: A man in a

Gordon Babb, posing

"I think of bodybuilding as a form, well, it's not a form of bal-let but it's very similar to ballet. To me, it seems like I've learned a lot from studying ballet move-ments and watching them. Going to see them with my wife. My wife is very interested in this so it's had an influence on me."
——Frank Zane

Frank & Christine Zane at home, Venice, Calif.

pair of trunks (you would be unusual if at the end of the routine you could remember what color they were) gets up on a posing dais under a spotlight, and for a minute or two he flexes and shifts his body into different positions. The positions are called poses or shots. A normal show routine would include around fifteen of them, though some bodybuilders who work very fast, like Franco Columbu, might get thirty into the same length of time. In the best routines there are no major body weaknesses to cover up, so the poses would be about equally divided among front, side and back shots. Some of these would be standards, and a few, like the back double-biceps and the hulking front pose called "most muscular" or "the crab," are almost obligatory. Others would be personal variations of standard poses, and if it were one of the very best routines you would also see one or two poses that belong to that bodybuilder alone—that, because he fills them in a way no one else can fill them or has filled them, are his, no matter how many other people do them. The kneeling three-quarter back pose belongs to Arnold Schwarzenegger in this way. Larry Scott, one of the greatest posers ever, owned the front single-biceps pose before he retired, and now, six or seven years later, he still owns it.

The poses you'd see, since they have no cheating in them and do not strain for emotion, would be dramatic without being melodramatic, their drama coming naturally from the imaginative sureness of their composition. Each one would both surprise and gratify you—would seem an inevitable yet altogether new disposition of the body. Each would have its own emotional weight and character and yet be integrally bound to all the others in the routine. And finally, each pose, as well as the whole routine, would seem transparent to you after it was over—as clear and simple as water.

Just as important as the poses themselves is the movement connecting them: all the best posing is an equal mixture of drama and grace, and it is the transitions that supply most of the grace. The movement in this routine would be unhurried, virile, smooth, carrying the body off the line of one pose just before the muscles begin to quiver from the strain of holding it, naturally and forcefully to the next. You would see no hesitation or thought; no stumbling or readjustment or compensation. All you would see is clear, lovely shifts, plunges and sweeps, some of them protracted and long-lined, others as choppy and brief as body punches, setting up the poses and carrying out of them again in what would seem to you the only possible way there is to do it.

A sense of things being done in the only way they can be done is one of the things you would feel, watching the routine; another is the clarity and impersonality of it. During very good posing you don't notice a bodybuilder's face any more than you do the color of his trunks. Neither do you, unless you are very new to watching, wonder what kind of man he is, or what he does for a living, or what his problems might be. In the AAU, the judges interview each of the Mr. America contestants before the competition, and the title is awarded partially on the basis of what they decide about—his character, or charm, some Atlantic City qualification that has nothing to do with what he is there for. The practice demeans bodybuilding competition and violates one of the things that is most unique and real about it: the fact that when both physique and posing are good enough they force the spectator to concentrate on a clean, impersonal, exciting geometry of circles and curves and on the movement tying it together, and to forget completely that it is a greased, nearly naked man, with charm or without, who is showing it to you.

The best posing is also completely without affectation or mannerisms. The way it was done by Grimek and Ross and Pearl and Scott, and the way it is done now by Arnold Schwarzenegger, Franco Columbu, Ed Corney and a few others, it seems, like all good art, artless. It isn't, of course; it is very highly contrived, but contrived in a way that blends grace and drama without any obtrusive magnification of either. That is the old way, the classic way, and in Corney and Schwarzenegger it may have reached its apogee.

There are two popular alternatives to that way now; both are flashier and easier to do, and both attract more and more young bodybuilders every year. One is a soft, choreographed kind of posing, much admired by women spectators. It is generally very graceful and melodramatic and is often performed to music. For its effects it relies on slow, mannered movements and moody, sinuous shots, many of them unflexed. Frank Zane is the leading proponent of this style. Zane is a nice man and an excellent bodybuilder with a small, beautifully proportioned physique that is as appropriate as any could be to this kind of posing. In his exhibitions he performs to music from *The Ten Commandments* and *2001*; and if, in watching, you get a slight sense of overripeness, of an overemphasis on grace, you at least know you are seeing this style of posing done as well as anybody does it.

The polar opposite of Zane's style is the one that, of present bodybuilders, Lou Ferrigno best represents. Ferrigno is six feet six and weighs around 275 pounds. Everything about him is enormous in the way boxcar couplings are enormous, and, of its kind, he has one of the best unfinished physiques in the history of bodybuilding. His posing (which is widely admired and copied in the East) is awesome and joyless, and lopsidedly dependent on his size. For his routine, Lou comes on stage looking angry and sleepy, as though the audience were a midnight burglar he'd surprised, and proceeds to crush out one massive shot after another. There is a sort of surly drama to what he does up there, but no more subtlety or grace than there is in the movement of road-building equipment.

Ferrigno is still in his early twenties, which is very young for a world-class bodybuilder. His potential is great, and it could be that his posing will take on art as his physique takes on finish, and that he will desert all the hulking, grimacing imitators he has now. It could also be that it won't. You can learn good posing only up to a certain point. Beyond that it is purely a matter of talent, and of intuition.

Arnold Schwarzenegger finished his routine, and the Olympia prejudging, with a crab shot that sent Raol into a frenzy of language behind us. Arnold grinned at the judges—it was the first time he had looked directly at them since he began—and left the stage without looking back, wiping down his shoulders and chest the way you do the flank of a lathered horse. Virginia and I sat for a couple of minutes without talking, she chewing on her lower lip and watching the ring of dampness that Arnold had left behind on the stage.

We had just seen a posing routine. In fact, we had just seen three—his, Franco's and Serge Nubret's—any one of which could serve, on film, say, as a wordless definition of what bodybuilding is all about.

Virginia shifted and laid her head back on the seat. It was the first move I'd seen her make in fifteen minutes.

"Why aren't they famous? Why doesn't everybody know about this?"

"They just haven't gotten around to it. And bodybuilding has given itself a rotten press. You ready to go? It's five-thirty."

"I feel like I was just hit in the eyes with a goddam ax."

"He'd like to hear that. Why don't we go backstage and you can tell him that."

"No. I don't want to meet him—just dream about him. It's sad, Chawes—that more people don't know. When you see it like that there's nothing, you know, *dingy* about it, or id-ish, or vain, or any of those things I thought it would be."

"The best ones do that for you. When they pose they cut right through all the myths and the bad organization and the tacky magazines, all that chalky feet stuff, and show you what the thing is really like."

"Chalky feet stuff?"

"It's just something I remember from when I first started going to these things."

"Did you like them then?"

"Not at first. I didn't know how to look as well as you do. We'd better move it if you're going out."

"They must be awfully lonely. Doing that beautiful thing and nobody around to appreciate it."

Frank Zane

"There are people around who do. There'll be a couple of thousand of them here tonight."

I stood up and handed Virginia her coat. She took it but didn't get up. She sat there with her lovely head on the back of the seat, looking up at me.

"Will he be that good tonight?"

"Maybe better. The Oak loves an audience."

"I've decided I'm going to come." She stood up then and put on her coat.

"I thought you couldn't."

"I can."

We walked up the aisle toward the dark front of the Brooklyn Academy of Music. Down on the stage they were setting up for the show. The bodybuilders would have a couple of hours now to go out and get something careful to eat, though most of them probably wouldn't.

"Chawes?" said Virginia. "You know what I said about Elizabethan music? Well, that was dumb. It's not a bit like that. Not at all."

Lou Ferrigno

Twelve
Mr. Olympia No. 4

Franco was nearly perfect. He was in the best shape of his life and he thought he could win, defeating the bar-fight maxim that a good big man will always beat a good small one. As it happened, he did beat one big man, and on another night he might have beaten the other one. But tonight Franco was followed not by another routine at all, but by an epiphany—a performance that revealed in the space of a couple of minutes, to everyone in the audience who was watching well enough, all there is to know about bodybuilding; allowed them to see it entire, like a pasture from a helicopter.

Like so much of what he does, in posing trunks and out of them, Arnold Schwarzenegger's routine that night turned on a single moment, a single brilliant intuition. He has a flair for them. Like earlier that day, for instance. At just about the same time Serge Nubret's limousine was pulling up in front of the Brooklyn Academy, the Oak turned off of Sixth Avenue onto Forty-fourth Street in mid-Manhattan and strolled down the block toward his hotel. The Algonquin Hotel to be exact—in whose small, exquisite lobby generations of literati have sat on the red sofas, ringing for tea or gin; in its dining room and lobby the Oak and the other bodybuilders staying there were pondered like literary symbols. It was a brilliant September morning, the rectangle of sky between the buildings on Forty-fourth Street was a hard enamel blue, and the air on the street crackled with light. The Oak turned the corner and walked down the block like a wave breaking. He was wearing emerald-green shorts. His centaur legs were a bright copper color from a new coat of Tan-

"I find out which poses they really like. That's why I don't have a specific posing routine, because you never know what they like and what they don't. Sometimes you think a routine is good but the applause is going down. Like Franco explained, he did one shot coming up for triceps from the side and the sound went down, so he cut the shot. You have to be very flexible in these things. You have to listen. When you hit the most-muscular and they start screaming, you know they like the more freaky poses, so you keep hitting it again and maybe hold it longer to get the cuts out more. You know then they like the drama shots and you can forget the symmetrical stuff."
——Arnold Schwarzenegger

"Not many bodybuilders dress up the way we do. The reason I dress up, it really makes me proud. And Natalie. I have my clothes tailored for myself, and I like to show. It's like you have a collection and it's part of you and you like to show people. It's my hard work—to keep my body in shape, and hers. And we like to dress up and we like to show. We go to a place and people talk and turn and they laugh about it and some of them make jokes about it, and all this makes us feel even more proud of it. There's no better thing than working with something that you really own. I can have a beautiful racing car and somebody can steal it, but your body—your body is the only thing you really own."
——Tony Roma

"Tony goes with me to ladies' stores because I like him to tell me what clothes I should put on, and they just laugh and laugh cuz they just can't stand the bodybuilders. And we in turn, we laugh at them because we know that that's so lousy. We just laugh at them . . . it's a ball. I have a ball every time we go out. Everyplace we go everybody stares at us like we're men from Mars or something like that. I think bodybuilding's a great thing. I'm really into it all the way, you know. I like watching men work out. And I help Tony all the time—I sit on his back for donkey calf-raises; I give him incentive."
——Natalie Raposa

Legs on 44th Street, New York

Tony Roma & Natalie Raposa, the Algonquin Hotel

in-a-Minute. A car full of his buddies turned onto Forty-fourth and slowed beside him, and then suddenly the whole street was alive with bodybuilders, driving up in cars, coming out of the hotel. The doorman and taxi drivers gaped: these huge people seemed conjured from the sparkling air. There was laughter from the car and a shout as it pulled off. Out in the street behind it the Oak whooped mightily and kicked at the fender. There were maybe a dozen pairs of eyes in front of the Algonquin Hotel, and all of them watched his carved leg wink outward in a high floating punt that seemed to catch the fancy New York morning smack in the bustle. It was a perfectly intuited fusion of moment with motion, of a physical act with a collective state of mind—as spontaneous and unpredictable as bodybuilding itself—and it cracked the instant open like an egg on a pan. Possibility ran in the street. Blasé, the Oak went upstairs to change. There was nothing new to him about this sort of labor; a couple of years ago he made a movie here called *Hercules in New York.*

So later, backstage at the Academy, listening to the crowd and knowing he needed something, some little exactly right something to follow Franco with, Arnold Schwarzenegger simply reached down and came up with it.

What happens is this:

In a madness of noise, an ear-splitting, wall-shaking tumult of noise, he takes the stage, his face radiant, and shows the audience and judges—a single leg. It is the leg he injured a few months earlier when a posing platform in South Africa collapsed with him, and he wants them to see that it is as good as ever. He turns it languidly, showing the elegant complexity of his calf. Then he cuts to a front double-biceps—a pose that shows the entire front of the body. From zoom to pan, from detail to mind-blowing whole. It's as sharp and right as that kick outside the hotel, and it impales the crowd. A sort of moaning begins out

"Number one, it runs through my mind it is very obvious that I am the king. Then I thought to the audience, just keep screaming now because you're going to see the poses for just a few minutes here, so eat your hearts out."
——Arnold Schwarzenegger

Mr. Olympia, 1973

front as they take in the softball-sized biceps, the long, deep pectoral slabs, the yawning latissimus dorsi—all that carved, intricate bulk at once. He holds it, his body straight, his arms flexed at shoulder height, a pure, lovely, demanding pose that demonstrates both his size and symmetry at once.

From there he goes in a crunch of arms to the most muscular, turning his chest, arms and shoulders into an anatomy-chart splay of veins and cuts, and maddening the audience. Then to his own three-quarter back shot, a one-arm side back, a back double-biceps, a side back with the other arm—each movement long, pure, uncluttered. It is posing at its driest and shapeliest, mixing grace and drama without cheating or excess and with no taint of the effete or the grotesque. It makes you feel, in the dignity and beauty of its finish, that you have never watched posing before.

And as he lays these perfect poses on the crowd, the luck and strain and glamour and joy of doing it are right up there on Arnold's face. All over his features. No preoccupation here, Jack, no dark, motivated, Nubretish absence of expression here. He is as into this as the ravening crowd—glistening, flexing, swooping from shot into marvelous shot. These are his people, and this is his thing, at his moment. He is Nureyev in London, Caruso at La Scala, Babe Ruth at Wrigley Field pointing his bat—a king, with a court, at the top of his art.

When he finishes with another most muscular, throws up his hands and bounds off the dais out of the spotlight, the deafening mixture of screaming, moaning and applause that has not sagged, not once, since he came out takes on a strangely wrenched quality, almost of lament. Nearly to the stage exit, Arnold stops in the half-dark. He listens to the audience, his head cocked, smiling in the shadows. Then he looks back at the dais, hesitates, and returns.